Dedicated to
my wife, Cathy,
who cheerfully visited many
Franciscan friary remains
with me

'Archbishop Peckham called the friars
"the wheels of God's chariot",
carrying God's message throughout the land.'

– John R. H. Moorman[1]

(Archbishop John Peckham lived c1230–1292,
and in addition to being Archbishop of Canterbury
he was Preserver of Privileges of the
Friars Minor in the English Province)

Reading's Grey Friars

Reading's Grey Friars

1233–1538

by
Malcolm Summers

About the author:

Malcolm Summers worked as a maths teacher for 36 years, 24 of them as a Deputy Head. Originally from Birmingham, he has lived in Reading for almost 40 years. He is married with two grown up children.

Also by the author:

History of Greyfriars Church, Reading – available from Greyfriars Bookshop, Reading

Nicolas Appert – a biography of the man who invented the process used to preserve food. Available from Amazon

Henry George Willink – a biography of the man after whom The Willink School is named. Available from Amazon

Signs of the Times: Reading's Memorials (Two Rivers Press) – available from booksellers in Reading and from tworiverspress.com

Published by Downs Way Publishing
1 Downs Way, Tilehurst, Reading RG31 6SL

ISBN 978-0-9927515-4-8

Photographs are by the author unless otherwise credited.

Chapter		Page

Cover photo:
Late 13th / Early 14th century head stop on the west wall,
Greyfriars Church, Reading.

Back cover:
Photograph of the author by Liffy Gorton

Friars are not monks

Friars and monks were and are very different. The monks appeared first: the earliest foundation in England was Augustine's in Canterbury in 598. The Benedictine abbey at Reading was founded in 1121, eighty-eight years before the Order of the friars minor, also known as the lesser brothers or Franciscans, was founded by St Francis of Assisi.

Monks had 'entered a religious house or monastery and had taken vows to remain there for the rest of their lives, and to cut themselves off from the life of the world while they devoted themselves to liturgical, scholastic and other kinds of work. A monk's main task was to perform what was called the *Opus Dei* which meant attendance at a daily course of services'.[2] His was the very definition of a cloistered life.

In contrast, a friar's vow of poverty, chastity and obedience did not cut him off from the world. The life of a friar involved him being among the people, mostly the poor, ministering to both their bodily and spiritual needs. Many friars were also preachers, popular with the crowds because they spoke in a plain and accessible way. They were evangelists, bringing the Good News of the Christian Gospel to people who were unlikely to hear it any other way.

Monks enjoyed a good standard of living for the time, within what was probably a wealthy religious house. Friars lived hand to mouth, eating only what local people had given them out of the kindness of their hearts. Most monks were only really seen during the divine services in their Church. Friars visited people's homes and brought them comfort and help whenever possible.

So, although easily confused, friars and monks are not the same at all.

*A Franciscan Frier minor, or Grey Frier
without his Mantle or Cloak.*

From *Collectanea Anglo-Minoritica*
by Anthony Parkinson
1726

Chapter 1

July 1233

One summer day in 1233 a small group of barefoot, ragged men, dressed in grey habits tied by a strangely knotted girdle, appeared in the market place at Reading. It is unlikely that anyone seeing them recognised them for what they were, as few of the town's residents would have previously met any friars of the Franciscan Order. Neither the names nor the number of these visitors are known, but they had probably lately come from the Oxford House, otherwise known as a friary, founded just over eight years earlier.

Passing beside St Laurence's Church, the friars would have entered Reading Abbey through the Compter Gate, its main entrance. This led into the Forbury, an open area inside the abbey's walls. Just inside the gate, the guest house known as the Hospitium of St John welcomed all. However, these men were not pilgrims looking for temporary shelter before moving on; they had arrived in this royal town with the full intention of staying and establishing a Reading House.

The friars sought an audience with the abbot, Adam de Lathbury. Adam had previously been prior of Leominster, a cell of Reading Abbey, and had been Reading's abbot since 1226. As abbot, he had welcomed King Henry III to the abbey several times, the first being for the Christmas season in the year he became abbot.[3] He had hosted the 5th General Chapter of the English Benedictine abbots the following year.[4] Adam would have been less pleased to see these visitors.

The Franciscans had been in England for less than ten years by this date, having probably arrived on 10 September

1224.[5] Francis of Assisi had formalised his *Ordo fratrum minorum*, the Order of the friars minor or lesser brethren, and been blessed with Pope Innocent III's approval in 1209. Since then large numbers of men had flocked to join the Order and as a result the organisation began to spread across Europe and on into Asia and Africa. In 1219 Francis appointed Agnellus of Pisa as the first Minister-Provincial of the yet-to-be-created province of England and commissioned him to take the Franciscan mission there.

Agnellus and eight other friars, three of whom were English, landed at Dover and lost no time in starting their work. The rapidity with which they flourished is quite astonishing. Within a year they had established friaries in Canterbury, London, Oxford, Northampton and Cambridge.

The next few years saw the friars expanding their mission east to Lincolnshire and Norfolk (at Norwich, King's Lynn, Lincoln and Stamford), north to the midlands (Leicester, Nottingham), to the west (Worcester, Hereford, Bristol and Gloucester) and south to Salisbury. It is possible that they reached Berwick as early as 1231.[6]

The grey friars were not the first religious community to settle in these places. Neither were they even the first friars to come to England: the Dominican or black friars had been here since 1221 and had established about ten houses by 1233. The number of friaries, however, paled into insignificance when compared with the very large number of monastic foundations, especially of the Benedictine order.

Many of the Franciscan friaries mentioned above had been founded with the financial assistance of local wealthy individuals. The king, Henry III, had also generously supported some with grants of land. However, the situation in Reading was one that the friars had not yet come across, since the abbey was the major landowner in the town and the abbot was Lord of the Manor of Reading.

In the 1220s there had not been any real opposition from

2

any monasteries to the settlement of the friars minor in any town. However, the 1230s were going to prove a different story. In the same year that the Reading House was founded, the grey friars tried to settle in Bury St Edmunds but faced vigorous opposition from the Benedictine monks of St Edmund's Abbey there. Having been forcibly removed from the town by the monks, the grey friars tried there again in 1257. They managed to hang on until 1262 before the monks finally made them leave the town. The friars settled in nearby Babwell safely out of the jurisdiction of the abbey.[7]

Later in the 1230s there were problems at Winchester, Chester and Scarborough. The story behind the opposition at Winchester is not known, but it is generally believed to have been opposition from the Benedictine monks there when the grey friars tried to settle in the city in 1237.

It was not monks but the Bishop of Coventry and Lichfield who protested against the grey friars settling in Chester in 1238. The Bishop, Alexander de Stavensby, argued that allowing the Franciscans would be injurious to the interests of the black friars, the Dominicans, who had preceded them there. His stand was opposed by no less a person than Bishop Robert Grosseteste, Bishop of Lincoln, former lector in theology to the Franciscans at Oxford, and a man of exceptional talent and understanding.

Grosseteste's carefully reasoned and impassioned appeal to his fellow prelate was followed by a letter from the king stating that he wished the Franciscans to be allowed to settle in Chester. This, of course, silenced all argument and the friary was soon established.[8]

In 1240, it was monks of the Cistercian Order who objected to the friars minor settling in Scarborough. As a result, the grey friars had to leave and it was not until thirty years later that they managed to move back and be established there.[9]

This antipathy between monks and friars had several roots.

They had very different ways of living a spiritual life. The former magnified God by service in church with much ceremony and magnificence; the latter served in poverty and with what we would term today social action. Monks may have looked down upon the beggarly friars, although some were challenged by their practical faith. It was not unknown for monks, in spite of their vow to their monastery, to 'change their coats' and become one of the grey friars. John of Reading is a good example of this. After six years as abbot of Osney Abbey, a house of Augustinian Canons, he joined the Northampton House of the friars minor in 1235, later moving to Oxford.[10]

A monastery looked to the local people for lay brothers and for a supply of novices. The establishment of a Franciscan House nearby would take some of those resources, possibly even cause a shortage since the friars were known to be popular with the common people. The monastery may have felt threatened by this.

Some of the reasons behind the opposition of the established monasteries to these newly arrived Franciscans were listed by the Augustinian Canons of Walsingham in a document written in the middle of the 14th century. A new friary had been proposed a short distance away from their Priory, and so they formalised their protest in a petition to Elizabeth de Burgh, Countess of Clare, whose intention it was to found the friary:

Among the arguments put forward were the prospective loss of tithes; that the friars would draw the parishioners away from their parish churches and by celebrating mass and hearing confessions would deprive the parish priest of his effective cure of souls; that the offerings at churchings of women and burials would "through the enticements, blandishments and deceptions of the friars", be lost to the church; that many other parochial rights would be infringed...[11]

Their final attempt to avoid having the new friary in their vicinity was to state that, as there were already houses of the Carmelite friars at Burnham, 4 miles away from Walsingham, and at Sniterley, 5 miles in another direction, no further house of friars was needed. Their opposition was not successful, however, as the Walsingham House was duly licenced by King Edward III and Pope Clement VI in 1347.

Back in 1233, it was clear that the newly arrived friars in Reading were well aware of the potential for difficulties in their relationship with the abbey as they came prepared. They presented abbot Adam with two letters, one from the abbot's spiritual superior, Pope Gregory IX, and one from his temporal master, King Henry III.[12] These letters desired the abbot to allow the friars to settle in the town.

In spite of this weighty pressure, Adam de Lathbury still took some convincing. A contemporary annal states that it was only 'through much insistence' that 'they obtained a place to live near the bridge of Reading from the reluctant abbot'.[13]

The land that was granted by the abbot did not become the property of the friars, but remained abbey land. This was due to the vow of poverty taken by the Franciscan friars. Neither individually nor corporately could any friar own anything. Friaries elsewhere were generally founded with a gift of land or buildings by one or more individuals who usually transferred ownership to the local Corporation in trust for the friars. The abbey, however, clearly did not wish to transfer ownership of a part of its land to anyone else.

Later in the 13th century, all Franciscan property became vested in the Pope. This situation was changed in 1322 by a decree of Pope John XXII, which altered the Rule of Poverty for Franciscans, allowing them corporately to own property.

On 14 July 1233, abbot Adam, having no doubt discussed the situation at length with the company of monks in the abbey's chapter, granted the grey friars land outside the

5

town's boundaries, near the road to Caversham. The grant began:[14]

> Enrolment of a deed, whereby the abbot and convent of Reading grant to the friars minors land in the culture called Vastern by the King's highway, towards the bridge of Caversham, measuring thirty-three perches in length and twenty-three perches in breadth, that they may there build and dwell, so long as they have no property ...

The land the abbey granted was therefore to the north of the town, probably in the area now bounded by Caversham Road on the west, Greyfriars Road on the east, Vachel Road on the south and Tudor Road on the north (see the map on page 17). This is down the hill from the location of the present Greyfriars Church, which we shall see in due course was a later addition and not the first friary church. Unfortunately, nothing remains of the original location of the friary buildings.

By 1233 there had been a bridge over the river Thames leading to Caversham for at least two years. The earliest reference to such a bridge is from 1231, where an entry in the Close Roll commands the Sheriff of Oxfordshire to:

> go in person taking with him good and lawful men of his county to the chapel of St Anne on the bridge at Reading over the Thames one side of which is built on the fee of the Abbot of Reading and the other on the fee of William Earl Marshall...[15]

The size of the land allowed to the friars is stated in the grant as 33 by 23 perches, but we cannot be certain that this was the same amount that we would now reckon it to be. If we use modern measurements, with a perch being a quarter of a chain, a perch is then 5½ yards, or 16½ feet (just over 5 metres). That would mean that the land was 181½ yards by

126½ yards, giving very nearly 4¾ acres (about 166m by 116m, giving 1.92 hectares).

However, the perch was subject to variation. In order to know what length is meant we either have to start with the measure of a foot, and then multiply by however many feet might be in a perch, or we start with the definition of an acre being the area that a team of oxen could plough in a day, and then work back to furlongs, chains and perches. None of these was standardised in the 13th century.

Nearly 40 years before this land grant, Richard I had made efforts to standardise the yard, but to no avail. Mention was made of standardisation of weights and measures in Magna Carta in 1215, particularly for wine, ale, corn and cloth. However, it did not achieve its object in terms of length as variation continued.[16] By the 16th century, the following working definition of a foot was printed:

> Stand at the door of a church on a Sunday and bid 16 men to stop, tall ones and small ones, as they happen to pass out when the service is finished; then make them put their left feet one behind the other, and the length thus obtained shall be a right and lawful rood [or perch] to measure and survey the land with, and the 16th part of it shall be the right and lawful foot.[17]

Note here that the perch is defined as 16 feet, not 16½. This illustrates the next problem, which was that the number of feet in a perch varied – often depending on the type or quality of land, whether it was woodland or pasture, rich soil or poor. As a result, a perch could vary from 9 to 24 feet. This gives us the possible variation of area from about 1½ to 10 acres (or 0.6 to 4 hectares)! Given that the land was wasteland and, as became apparent, subject to periodic flooding, it is likely that the measure used would be towards the more generous end and so giving about 6 or 7 acres as we would now measure them.

The abbot's grant of land was hedged about with clauses to ensure that the Franciscans knew who was in charge. The next part of the grant showed that the Benedictines were well aware of the vow of poverty that the friars had taken:

> ...and the friars minors agree that if at any time they have property or aught of their own, the abbot and convent may eject them from the said land without contradiction or appeal; and that they will never require any other dwelling place on the lands of the abbey or endeavour to enlarge their house, upon the same penalty; nor will they ever require any support from the said abbot and convent, save what is freely given to them, upon the same penalty;

The friars could be sure that the abbey would be on the look out to catch them out in terms of ownership of 'aught of their own'. Not much brotherly love was being shown by the abbey when they stated that the penalty for getting it wrong would be expulsion from the land without contradiction or appeal.

The remaining areas of concern to the abbey were to limit the friars' abilities to raise money at the expense of the abbey and its rights. The grant continued:

> ...nor will they bury in their graveyard at Reading any bodies but those of friars minors without special licence of the abbot and convent, upon the same penalty; nor shall they take any offerings, legacies or tithes due to the abbot and convent, upon the same penalty;

The people had such a belief in the holiness of the grey friars that it became popular for those who were able to afford it to pay to have themselves buried in a friars' church or its burial ground, and if possible dressed in the habit of a friar. This was seen as gaining holiness by association, leading to a significant remission of time needing to be spent atoning for sins in Purgatory, especially as they expected to count on the intercession of St Francis himself.[18]

However, this clause of the grant would not have troubled the abbot or the friars for a while, as the first burial of a lay person that is recorded in an English friary church was from forty years later. It was the burial of the heart of Richard, Earl of Cornwall, at the church of the Grey Friars at Oxford in 1272.[19]

The abbey's grant then gave the friars some assurances:

> ...but if the abbot and convent expel them on any other ground than those above recited, the king shall cause the said friars minors to possess the said land, so that they shall hold of his grace what they held of the grace of the abbot and convent;

This looks only reasonable at first sight. However, it caused difficulties when Albert of Pisa became the third Minister-Provincial of the Friars Minor, that is the leader of the Franciscans in England, in 1236. When he read the document, his reaction was immediate. In *The Chronicle of Thomas of Eccleston* written about 20 years later, the author said that Albert:

> with great fervour of spirit ... returned to the monks of Reading the writing or agreement whereby they bound themselves not to expel the brethren [friars] at their own will. He even offered, should the monks desire it, himself to remove the brethren.[20]

What caused Albert to be horrified was the possibility of circumstances that could lead to the situation where the friars might 'possess the said land'. It might have been unlikely to happen, but Albert did not want there to be any chance of the friars falling foul of their Vow of Poverty. It would seem to me that he need not have worried, as the clause 'they shall hold of his grace what they held of the grace of the abbot and convent' looks to provide for the ownership to pass to the king, and not to the friars. Fortunately for the friary, however, Adam de Lathbury did not take the opportunity of removing the friars that Albert offered him.

The grant concluded:

> ...but if ever the said friars minors abandon their said habitation, the land and all the buildings thereon shall revert to the said abbot and convent; of all which a chirograph has been made and the part remaining with the abbot and convent sealed with the common seal of the minors in England, and with the seal of the king and with the seals of the archbishop of York, and the bishops of Winchester, Coventry, and Worcester; dated A.D. 1233, at Reading, 14 July.

A chirograph was a document written in duplicate on one piece of parchment which had the word *chirographum* written across the middle. The parchment was then cut in two, usually with a serrated or wavy line, and each party to the agreement kept a copy. These parts could be seen to be genuine by the fact that they could fit together back into one piece, with matching pattern.

The list of the seals attached to the document is impressive. It represents quite a gathering at Reading Abbey on that day in July 1233.

Chapter 2

The First Reading Friary

Early Franciscan friary buildings in England tended to be very simple affairs, usually constructed from wood or from wattle and daub. It was not until towards the end of the 13th century that their churches began to be made of stone.[21]

The Salisbury House is a good example of this. Founded in the late 1220s, the friary church and its other buildings were built of wood. By 1290 some of the wooden buildings needed to be replaced, and the new church was built using stone.[22] Similarly, the first Reading House, built in the 1230s, would have been of wooden construction.

The friars would have borne in mind the clear instructions from St Francis, although as time went on the message faded from memory:

> St Francis in a conversation with a benefactor described the method that his brethren should adopt when a piece of land was given to them to build a friary upon. Having obtained the blessing of the bishop of the diocese, they were to make a deep ditch around the land with a good fence instead of a wall as an emblem of their poverty; their cottages were to be of mud and wood, with some few cells for the friars to pray and labour in for the eschewing of idleness. They were to have small churches and not large ones. These poor houses, cells and churches would be their best sermons.[23]

Fresh from their success in being granted land by the abbey, the friars started work on their House. Meanwhile they needed a roof over their head. Elsewhere, the grey friars could count on a welcome and hospitality from the Dominican friars (the black friars, or preaching friars), but there was no settlement of Dominicans in Reading.

The likely accommodation for these new arrivals would have been a house, or part thereof, given to them for the time being by a generous townsperson. Failing that they would have had to rent a house, and add the expense of the rent to the amount they had to beg each day.

Since the friars had no money to buy anything, the cost of all the building materials would need to have been given to them. There were no doubt many gifts from liberal townspeople, but unfortunately no information of the donors is known, except for the records of the significant help provided by King Henry III. Writing of the Oxford friary, the Franciscan scholar A. G. Little wrote: 'No English king bestowed on the house of Franciscans at Oxford that loving care which Henry III bestowed on the Minorite Church at Reading'.[24]

From the records, in the Chancery Calendars of Close Rolls and of Liberate Rolls of Henry's reign, we can gather both the progress and something of the scope of the work done.

The first recorded gift by the king to the friars was on 2 May 1234. It allowed them 'without hindrance and any chiminage [a toll for passing through the forest] to be able to remove until the feast of St Michael this year timber that shall be given them from the forest of Windles [Windsor] for their buildings to be erected in Reading'.[25]

Whatever progress the friars had made since the previous July, this gift of timber would ensure that they could make good headway throughout the summer and autumn of 1234, until the Michaelmas (29 September) deadline.

By the end of June 1234 they had built the walls of the church, which was most probably just rectangular. The king again showed his desire to benefit the Franciscans by giving them the necessary wood for the roof:

> For the friars minor of Reading. – Gileberto de Everle was commanded to provide the brothers of the minor order of Reading seventy oaks from the forest of Penbergh [Pamber], to make the rafters in the church, by gift of the king.
> Witnessed by the king at Keniton, 28th June [1234][26]

The church was probably in use from soon after this date. More will be said about the type of church the Franciscans built when we come to the present building after the 1285 grant of further land (see the next chapter). Here, it will be sufficient to note that in the early to middle years of the 13th century, Franciscan friars built all their churches on fairly similar patterns, with a rectangle for the nave to the west, and a rectangle for the quire or chancel to the east, with no structure between the two, unlike their later churches. Neither the nave nor the quire would be likely to have had aisles.[27]

Several further gifts from Henry III improved the church over the following years. In August 1237 the king commanded the sheriff of Berkshire, Simon de Lewknor, to wainscot the 'chapel of the Friars Minors at Rading'.[28]

In the following April, when on a visit to Reading and no doubt staying at the abbey, Henry III instructed the new sheriff of Berkshire, Engelard de Cigoné, to have 'felled, trimmed and carried to the friars' House in Rading' three oaks for their choir stalls.[29]

Over a year later, however, the choir stalls were still unfinished. On 1 August 1239 the king directed the next sheriff of Berkshire, Hugh le Despenser, to 'cause the stalls of the friars minors at Rading in their church to be completed, and to cause two altars to be made in the chapel'.[30]

As well as paying for these two altars, the king funded their decoration. Hugh le Despenser was to 'cause a board for the altar painted and starred with gold to be made for [the friars'] use'.[31]

We have two confirmations that this decorative work was completed. First, six months later, the sheriff was paid '12 marks 9s 2d' from the king's treasury for carrying out this work.[32] A mark was two thirds of a pound, and so 12 marks equalled £8.

The second way that we know this work was carried out was from the reaction of the Minister-Provincial of England, Albert of Pisa, a man who had known St Francis of Assisi personally. He was not only zealous that the friars minor should not own anything individually or corporately, as we saw in chapter 1, but also that the brethren should live in simplicity and poverty, not surrounded by signs of wealth or expense. He had had the stone cloister erected by the burgesses at Southampton pulled down, much against the will of the townspeople, because he thought it too grand.[33] This gold-starred altar at Reading was also beyond the pale, but because it was a gift from the king, Albert could do nothing about it, except that 'he earnestly prayed that Heaven would destroy it'.[34]

This was not the last of Henry's efforts to add to the glory of the friary church. In 1246 he granted the friars 40s (£2) 'of the king's gift for the fabric of their church out of the amercements [fines] of the eyre [circuit court] of Robert Passelewe and his fellows, the last justices itinerant in the county for pleas of the forest'.[35]

In 1239, we obtain our first information about the number of friars at the Reading House. This is again as a result of King Henry's generosity. The sheriff of Berkshire, Hugh le Despenser, was to 'cause to be bought 52 ells of russet to make tunics for the use of thirteen friars minors at Reading, to wit 11d an ell at the most'.[36] This matches the usual measure, that a friar's habit was made from 4 ells of material. An ell, incidentally, is the length of a man's arm.

This number of friars at the Reading House, one warden and 12 friars, was the smallest that was permitted in the Order, although at least two Houses in Scotland, at Dumfries and Roxburgh, had only about 4 or 5 friars each.[37]

Many friaries were much larger. In 1256 there were, in the Province of England, 49 Houses and 'the number [of friars] dwelling therein was one thousand two hundred and forty-two'.[38] This yields an average per House of 25. As examples of the larger Houses in the mid-13th century, London and Oxford each had about 80 friars, Cambridge 70, Canterbury 60, and Norwich 50.[39]

As well as enabling us to know how many friars lived at the Reading House, the king's gift of 52 ells of russet leads us on to further discoveries. The cost, limited to 11 pennies an ell, represented cheap material, as the usual price at the time was 1s 4d (therefore 16d) an ell.[40] This followed the Rule of the Order, which specified that 'all the friars shall be clothed in coarse garments'.[41]

The material that the king paid for was russet. This was a cloth made from wool and dyed either a grey or a brown colour. It was likely that the friars wore russet dyed grey rather than brown, given their sobriquet of grey friars! The modern Franciscan habit is more frequently brown than grey.

The friary had at least six buildings: church, chapter house, dormitory (or dorter), 'privy chamber', refectory (or frater) and infirmary, as these are all mentioned in the records of the king's gifts. It was likely to have also had a building to accommodate guests, but this does not appear in the records.

In addition to these buildings, there would have been a cloister, which would have been the main area that linked all the other buildings together. Then there would have been the friary's grounds and gardens – we know that there was a pond, and later an orchard – all surrounded by a perimeter ditch and wooden palisade[42] and with a gated entrance onto the road to Caversham.

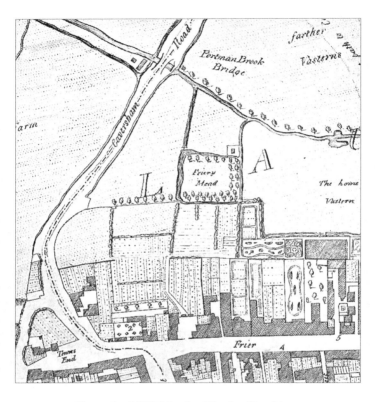

From the 1802 Map by Charles Tomkins
The Portman Brook is shown diverted around 'Friery Mead',
which is likely to have been within the grounds
of the first friary.

The later friary church can be seen in the lower left
(numbered 2) at a time when it was a Bridewell, or prison,
with just the dots of the columns showing as the roof had been
removed in the latter part of the eighteenth century.

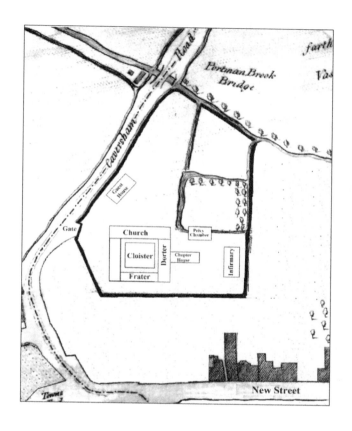

First friary imagined

This reconstruction uses features in the landscape
from the 1802 map opposite

The thick black outline shows the perimeter ditch and palisade

For the first few years from 1233, the friars either used sleeping accommodation in the town, or built a temporary shelter in their grounds. In autumn 1239 Henry III gave instruction to his sheriff of Berkshire, Hugh le Despenser, 'to cause to be built a dortour [dormitory] and chapter house for the friars minors at Rading at the pond'.[43] Note that this was not just the provision of wood, but assistance in the construction.

In a record in the Liberate Rolls that is partly lost or illegible, the king instructed that both the friary dormitory and the chapel were to have a storey added.[44] In the light of the issue of flooding that was complained of later, this suggests that the accommodation needed to go up a floor to avoid the problem.

On another visit to Reading, in December 1241, the king repaid Hugh le Despenser '50 marks spent on a privy chamber in two stories made for the friars minors of Rading; and 100s for clothing them during this year'.[45] The privy chamber would have been built over a source of running water. The Portman Brook was the nearest such source. The map on the previous page shows the Portman Brook diverted, probably for the purpose of serving the privy chamber as well as irrigating the land. The Portman Brook, known now as the Vastern Ditch, is mostly underground. It is culverted under Caversham Road approximately where the railway bridge crosses.[46]

Incidentally, the 100s (£5) given by the king for clothing the 13 friars would have paid for 2 habits each. At a cost of 11d per ell, and 4 ells per habit, material for 26 habits would have cost 95s 4d. Perhaps the extra 4s 8d funded a hood for one habit per friar, as the Order's Rule specified that the friars were allowed one habit with a hood and one without.[47]

The frater, or refectory, was the next building to be improved. In May 1244, when he was again in Reading, Henry commanded Hugh le Despenser to 'raise the walls of the refectory of the friars minors of Rading to make 3 large permanent windows in the roof besides the one already there, and a proper pulpit in the middle of the refectory, and to roof it well with shingles'.[48]

As this shows, in common with the other orders of both monks and friars, there was a reading while the brothers ate in the refectory. This reading would have been from the bible, or a life of a saint, or other similar spiritually uplifting source.

The raising of the frater's walls not only meant that three windows could be put in the roof, but also was probably to enable the friars to lift the level of the floor in order to avoid the effects of flooding. The shingles for the roof were most probably made from wood as four years later the king gave instructions that it should be tiled.[49]

The infirmary was built by this time, as in 1246 the king gave an order for a fireplace to be built there. He also instructed that a wall should be built between the infirmary and the privy chambers.[50] It seems a strange idea to have built the infirmary in the first place without a fire, but it may have seemed a luxury to the friars and so have been something they could not justify. The wall must have provided a sheltered walkway from the infirmary to the privy chamber.

Henry III continued over many years generously to give money and resources to the friary. Scattered throughout that time are numerous gifts of wood from the various royal forests, for building as we have already seen, and also for firewood. For example, on the same occasion in 1244 that the king ordered that the walls of the refectory should be raised, he told the sheriff of Berkshire to:

carry 4 logs, which the king has given to the same friars in the forest of Windes [Windsor] for fuel, to their house at Rading. Mandate to the constable of Windes to let them have the logs where they may be taken with the least damage to the forest and the most convenience to the friars.[51]

Two months later, it seems that the friars had either not received or not collected their wood, as the above instruction was cancelled and replaced with the command to the sheriff of Berkshire to 'buy brushwood to the value of 5 marks [£3 6s 8d] for the friars minors of Rading in lieu of 4 logs which the king granted them in the forest of Windes'.[52]

In 1247 the king instructed Henry de Farleg, Warden of Windsor Forest, to let the friars of Reading have 4 oak trunks from the forest of Penberch, or Pamber.[53]

It was not until June 1257 that the next grant of wood was made: 5 oak trunks from Windsor forest.[54] For some reason, the friars had only collected or received from Henry de Farleg two of the oak trunks by August of the following year. Perhaps they had been denied the remaining three oaks, as by this time Henry de Farleg had been replaced as Warden of Windsor Forest by Godfrey of Lyston. By a lucky circumstance, the king came to Reading that August, no doubt allowing the friars to make representation to him about the situation. Godfrey was instructed to ensure that the friars had the remaining wood.[55]

Not long after this, Henry was fully occupied with difficulties with his barons, led by Simon de Montfort, resulting in the Provisions of Oxford in 1258 and subsequently the Barons' War in 1264–1267. In the last thirteen years of Henry's reign before his death aged 65 in November 1272, he made just two further grants to the Reading House.

The first was in March 1259, allowing the friars six oaks from Windsor forest to repair a roof.[56] The second was for a further six oaks to shingle a roof in September 1260.[57]

With the passing of Henry, a golden age for the Franciscan Houses in England passed too. Never again would a king show so much favour to the friars. It was of course another Henry, the eighth of that name, who brought their Houses to their sudden end.

Chapter 3

The Second Reading Friary

It was almost eight years into Edward I's reign that the king first took notice of the Reading grey friars. In June 1280 he instructed the keeper of Pamber Forest to allow the 'friars minor of Reading to have three oak trunks for fuel, of the king's gift'.[58]

By this time the friary was almost 50 years old. There had been evident disadvantages of the site from quite early on due to periodic flooding. The land was mostly low-lying and, being near the Thames, was very prone to flooding. For example, in 1240, 'because of frequent floods', stated the *Annals of Reading Abbey*, 'half the bridge between the vill of Reading and Caversham was almost destroyed and collapsed'.[59]

The effect of the flooding is also shown by the need to add another floor to several of their buildings. The floods would also have affected the road into the town, making not just the friars' accommodation difficult but also the journey into Reading, where the friars needed both to minister and to beg for their daily sustenance.

The earliest expression of the need to move the friary in extant documents is in the letters of the Archbishop of Canterbury, John Peckham, in 1282. Like the Reading House, Peckham was about 50 years old. He was a Franciscan friar himself, probably since he was aged 20. He had studied at Paris University under the famous Bonaventure, who later became the seventh Minister-General of the Order of the Friars Minor, that is the overall leader of the Franciscans.

Peckham, after teaching for a while at the Franciscan seat of learning at the University of Oxford, became the Minister-Provincial of England of the Friars Minor in 1275.

Peckham was then consecrated as Archbishop of Canterbury by Pope Nicholas III in Rome in January 1279. Upon his arrival back in England, Peckham's first act was to call a Provincial Council of Bishops, choosing Reading for the meeting place. This Council, on 31 July 1279, probably took place in the abbey chapter house.[60] If Peckham had not been familiar with the Reading House of grey friars before, it would be surprising if he did not visit it at this opportunity.

About this time, the friars of Reading wrote a complaint about their friary's site to Cardinal Mattheo Orsini, who had been Cardinal Protector of the Franciscan Order, by order of Pope Nicholas III (his uncle), since 1277. Orsini then wrote to Peckham, passing on the details of the complaint.

In his turn, Peckham wrote to the abbot of Reading Abbey, Robert of Burgate, in September 1282 both as 'Archbishop of Canterbury, primate of all England, and the Preserver of the Privileges of the Friars Minor'. He brought to Robert's attention that the friary land was liable to periodic flooding in winter and that this resulted in serious inconvenience for the friars. Peckham noted that the original agreement that had been made between the abbey and the friars meant that the area of land should not be enlarged, but nevertheless he beseeched them, by the love of the blessed Saint Francis, to increase it.[61]

Peckham later wrote to the Minister-General of the Order of Friars Minor, Arlotto of Prato, whom he calls 'Brother Allot'. Coates, in his 1802 *History of Reading* gave the substance of Peckham's letter:

The archbishop [Peckham] informs him [Brother Allot] that the primitive simplicity of the friars in the province of England, as both in their choice of situations, and in erecting of buildings, they had shewn more eagerness than prudence, had produced much inconvenience to posterity; for necessity frequently compelled them to change their situations, and repair buildings which had fallen into decay. That the friars at Reading, compelled by the monks who had the chief authority there, had accepted a marshy situation, out of town, very subject to floods; that, in the time of an inundation, they were obliged to quit the place, or to remain there in great danger; and that in winter the distance from the town made it very inconvenient for them to procure necessaries. The archbishop adds, that, being solicited by many persons of consequence, the monks had at length given permission for the friars to enlarge the area of their building, and place it on higher ground within the precinct of the town.[62]

This letter from Peckham to Arlotto of Prato was to seek his seal of approval for the grant of additional land by the abbey. It had taken abbot Robert of Burgate until 1285 to succumb to the Archbishop and the 'many persons of consequence' and agree the extension. As in 1233, no detail was omitted by the abbot. The abbey's grant stated:

Enrolment of deed by R. abbot of Reading, and the convent of the same, witnessing that they have unanimously received as guests in the following manner the friars minors in their town of Reading upon a piece of ground between the house of Sir Stephen the chaplain, then rector of the church of Sulham, on the east and the sandy ditch on the west, and extending from the common way called New Street to the end of the piece of ground, the use whereof the friars have hitherto had and have and shall have henceforth of the abbot and convent's grace, saving the conditions specified below. The piece of land in question contains sixteen perches in breadth and sixteen and a half perches in length.

It shall be lawful for the friars to build and dwell upon the land for so long as they shall be without property and shall be, in accordance with their profession, observers of the deepest poverty. The friars have promised, for themselves and their successors, that they will never seek any other dwelling on the abbot and convent's land, or extend by themselves the boundaries aforesaid, or procure their extension by others, and that they will never seek alms from the abbot and convent as a due but only out of mercy and by special grace. They have also promised that whatsoever liberty of sepulture they enjoy or shall hereafter enjoy, they shall never receive for burial in their cemetery or church or elsewhere the bodies of deceased parishioners of the monastery or of the churches appropriated to the abbot and convent in the town of Reading or outside without the special licence of the abbot and convent, and that in this they will wholly abstain from prejudicing the abbot and convent and their men; and that they shall never receive tithes or offerings or legacies that are due of certain knowledge to the abbot and convent's church or by custom.

The friars have granted that if they fail in any of these articles with full knowledge or contravene them, the abbot and convent shall have power to expel them from the ground aforesaid by their own authority, any obstacle of appeal or contradiction being waived. If the abbot and convent shall wish to expel the friars from dwelling on the said land for any other causes than those expressed above, the king and heirs shall have free power to house them there, all appeal and contradiction being waived, so that they shall have of his grace the use that they previously had of the abbot and convent's grace. For corroboration the seals of the abbot and convent, on the one side, and the seals of the ministers general and provincial, on the other, together with the seal of the king and the seal of the archbishop of Canterbury are appended to this deed. Done at Reading, 7 Kal. June, 1285.[63]

The document's date is 7th before the kalends of June 1285. The kalends of June means 1st June, and so the 7th before it gives us the date: 25 May 1285. It is from this date, therefore, that the history of the second Reading House of Grey Friars begins. In due course, the new church would be built in stone and much of this still remains in the current Greyfriars Church.

This new plot of ground brought the friary up to the edge of Reading, in an area long known as Towns End and fronting onto 'the common way called New Street', which in time became known as Fryers Street and then Friar Street.

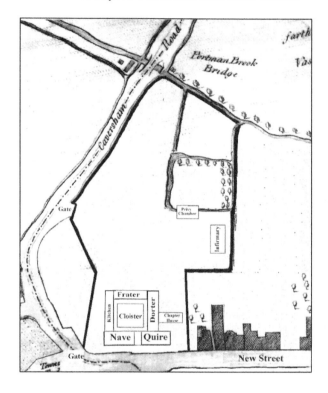

The extension to the friary grounds
showing the location of the new church
(Nave and Quire separated by a bell tower and walking place)

This is an imagined building plan; there are no traces left
showing any positions apart from the church.
The privy chamber and infirmary would also
be moved in due course.

The grant described the additional piece of land as adjoining the one the friary already stood on. The additional area, 16 perches by 16½, added just over a third again to the area of the friary. If we take a perch to be the modern value, then the extra land was over 1½ acres, bringing the whole to just under 6½ acres (about 2.6 hectares).

The conditions laid down by Abbot Robert of Burgate were the same as in the previous grant, albeit with more detail in places. For example, the part regarding burials is much more specific: in 1233 the condition was 'nor will they bury in their graveyard at Reading any bodies but those of friars minors without special licence of the abbot and convent, upon the same penalty' (i.e. expulsion from the site). In 1285 this had become: 'they shall never receive for burial in their cemetery or church or elsewhere the bodies of deceased parishioners of the monastery or of the churches appropriated to the abbot and convent in the town of Reading or outside without the special licence of the abbot and convent, and that in this they will wholly abstain from prejudicing the abbot and convent and their men'.

The deed had an impressive list of seals attached:
- Abbot of Reading Abbey, Robert of Burgate
- Convent of Reading Abbey
- Minister-General of the Order of Friars Minor, Arlotto of Prato
- Minister-Provincial of England of the Order of Friars Minor, Robert de Cruce (or possibly his successor from later in 1285, William of Gainsborough)
- Archbishop of Canterbury, John Peckham
- King Edward I

If it was surprising that the abbey allowed the friars this extra land, it was even more astonishing that just three years later, in 1288, there came no objection to a gift to the friary of some other pieces of land. This gift came from a bequest from

Robert Fulco, King's Justice in Reading.

Fulco appears several times in Reading documents of the 13th century, as both a giver and receiver of lands and buildings. He gained the trust of the king, who appointed him Royal Justice-in-Eyre for the town in 1280. Fulco had died by 8 September 1287, as on that date his executors, Roland of Erle (or Earley), Robert of Preston, Walter Fachel (or Vachel) and Ralph of Barford (or Beresford) sought permission of the king to have control of Fulco's estate.[64]

The four executors carried out Fulco's will, including selling off all his houses in Reading and distributing the money among the poor for the benefit of Fulco's soul. The friary received, as Coates puts it, 'certain void pieces of ground, in New Street, now Frier-street, adjoining to their former possessions'.[65]

From the day that the friars took possession of their extended ground in May 1285 they would have started work on a new set of buildings. Unfortunately, very little is known of these buildings or their locations. There are tantalising references to their remains but nothing that allows us to be specific about them.

The friary remains are mentioned by Mary Russell Mitford in her 1835 novel *Belford Regis or Sketches of a Country Town*, her thinly disguised description of her home town of Reading. Although this is a work of fiction, her detailed descriptions of local places are from life. She described the friary church as 'the most beautiful ruin in Belford' and places one of her character's cottages ('Friary cottage') among the 'fallen masses' of the other buildings. The closest she gets to any detail is when Louis Duval 'was sitting among the ruins as usual, one fine morning early in May, attempting for the twentieth time to imitate on paper the picturesque forms, and the contrasting yet harmonious colouring of a broken arch'. Elsewhere she describes the ruins as a 'favourite rendezvous with the inhabitants of Belford – a walk for the grown-up, a playground for the children'.[66]

In reality, rather than fiction, in September 1859 members of the British Archaeological Association visited Reading as an expedition from their Congress being held at Newbury. They visited the friary as part of their busy itinerary:

> ...when the Association proceeded thither, and found parts of it occupied as a gaol, and steps in contemplation for destroying it, lamentations were strongly expressed. It belongs to the thirteenth and fourteenth centuries, and displays a fine imbricated window. Mr Godwin urged the duty devolving upon the authorities of a rising town like Reading of preserving those ancient buildings which remained within it, and, deploring the fact that there was no museum in the town, suggested that the friary should be restored, and so appropriated, if a church were not needed.
>
> Messrs. Poulton and Woodman showed by a plan they had prepared, the existence of various foundations around indicating the extent of the establishment originally.[67]

Unfortunately, I can find no further details of this plan drawn up by Messrs Poulton and Woodman, who were architects based at 1 Greyfriars Road, and to whom was entrusted the restoration of the church in 1862.[68]

There is a further reference to the foundations of the friary buildings in the biography of the Rev W W Phelps, the man behind the restoration of the church. Referring to the visit by the British Archaeological Association, his biographer wrote:

> The foundations of the other conventual buildings were laid open for inspection by the archaeological society to be mentioned presently; they are on the north side of the church and at some distance from it.[69]

In 1285, one of the friars' first tasks would have been to fence the whole extended site around and erect a new gate.

Unlike for their first site, when a wooden palisade and ditch marked off the property's perimeter, this would have been a stone wall. The gate would have been at the New Street (Friar Street) end of the property, probably close to where the entrance to Greyfriars Church from the road is today. The gate is shown clearly on the 1611 map of Reading by John Speed as still existing some 70 years after the dissolution of the friary (see page 32).

The only surviving Franciscan gates in England.
At Dunwich, Suffolk

The new church building was made of stone, making use of the abundance of local flint stones. It was built at the very top of the hill, next to Friar Street. It was ready for its roof in 1303, as on 11 January that year King Edward wrote:

> To John de London, constable of Windsor castle and keeper of the king's forest there. Order to permit the friars minors of Redyng to fell and carry whither they wish fifty-six oaks fit for

timber in the wood of Henry de Lacy, earl of Lincoln, at Asherigge [probably Ashridge, near Wokingham], which is within the bounds of the king's forest of Windsor, as the earl has given them the said oaks.[70]

When the church had been roofed no doubt there was still much more work to do to complete the building. It may not have been very long after this date, however, that it was at least usable if not actually finished.

The completion date of the building of the church, cloister, frater, dorter, and so on, is not actually known. It is, however, frequently taken as 1311, following Coates' history of the town which stated that the buildings were not completed before 1311.[71] Almost everyone who has written about Greyfriars since has stated, with unannotated assurance, that the church was either built in or finished in 1311.

This date was chosen by Coates because of a phrase in the Last Will and Testament of 'Alanus de Bannebury', otherwise known as Alan of Banbury. This Will is dated on the Thursday after the feast of All Saints in 1311, which is usually taken to be 4 November 1311.[72]

Alan left the majority of his estate to his wife Christine and their daughter Margery. He left his hat shop to John le Cave of Blewbury, one of his executors, although the contents of the shop were not included – they were to go to his wife and daughter. The larger of the remaining bequests were 12s. for his funeral expenses, 10s. for bread to be distributed to poor people at his burial, and 5s. to the Reading friars minor.

The Latin phrase used is *operi fratrum minorum Radyngie,* which has been variously translated as 'for the work' or 'for the building' or 'for the use' of the friars minor of Reading. The implication could be that the building works were not as yet finished – hence Coates saying that the buildings were not completed before this date. If this is so, then the date of completion was 1311 or later. However, there is no way of knowing if this was a reference to the church itself, or to other friary buildings, so even if it does mean that the buildings were not completed at this point, the church may already have been finished before this date.

However, it is also possible that it was a phrase meant to imply that this money was given to support the good works of the friars as they ministered to the people of the town. If so, then this reference says nothing about the buildings, complete or otherwise.

All we can really say with any certainty is that the church walls, windows (although not necessarily their glass) and columns were in place by 1303, as the wood for the roof was given then. Since those are the parts of the church that remain from that date, perhaps that is all we need to know! The actual completion of the church building could have been relatively soon after 1303, or it may have taken several more years.

Perhaps after all 1311 is not too inaccurate a date to use, as long as we remember that in fact the date is not precisely known.

Above: The friary, from John Speed's map of Reading 1610

Detail of the friary church:
The nave is just behind the friary's gate.
The bell tower above the walking place is shown clearly,
with the quire or chancel to the right

Chapter 4

The Friary Church

The building that remains and is in use as a parish church today, was originally the aisled nave of the friary church. To the east was a chancel or quire, which was not aisled, but was likely to have been a similar width to the central nave, between the columns.

The most unusual feature of friary churches was that there was, between the nave and the quire, a corridor across the church called the walking place, opening out both onto Friar Street to the south and to the friary grounds to the north, and into the nave to the west and the quire to the east. Above this central corridor there was a bell tower, with at least two bells to toll the hours of divine services.

The early 17th century map of Reading by John Speed, opposite, gives a representation of the building over 70 years after its dissolution. It is not necessarily an accurate drawing of the friary, but it shows the general impression.

The lower drawing opposite is an enlargement of the church and gate from John Speed's map, showing the bell tower and the two parts of the church, a somewhat shortened nave to the left and the quire or chancel to the right.

There are three Franciscan bell towers still in existence in England: at Richmond in Yorkshire, in Coventry and in King's Lynn. To illustrate the likely type of structure at the Reading House, the next page shows photographs of the 15th century rectangular tower at Richmond, the late 14th century hexagonal tower at King's Lynn, and the mid-14th century octagonal tower at Coventry, which is surmounted by the much later addition of a spire.

Above: Richmond, Yorkshire

Below: King's Lynn, Norfolk

Above: Coventry,
West Midlands

View through the walking place,
with the nave to the left and the quire to the right.
Richmond, Yorkshire

As can be seen from the photograph above, the walking place cut the nave off from the quire. There were usually walls at both the east end of the nave and the west end of the quire, with a door in each. This made the quire a private chapel for the friars, with the public only allowed in the nave.

There is a drawing by John Chessell Buckler of the east wall of Greyfriars when it was a Bridewell, or Town prison, in 1860. This was just two years before the work began on the restoration of the building as a church, at which point the east wall was entirely rebuilt because it was unsafe. This drawing is probably the only surviving record of what the central part of the east wall of the friary nave looked like, showing the doorway into the walking place.

The drawing is in a bound volume of Buckler's architectural drawings, kept in the Western Manuscripts collection of the British Library.[73] Entitled *Stone Screen between the nave and choir of the Church of Grey Friars, Reading – 1860*, it shows a central doorway, 4ft 8in (1.42m) wide and 7ft 7½in (2.32m) tall, with a 3in (8cm) step up from the nave. On each side of the doorway there was a single column, topped by a decorative capital. The measurements on the drawing give the width of the whole chancel arch to be 18ft 8in (5.73m). The rest of the east wall was of brick and stone, so the screen was not a decorative tracery that could be seen through, but simply a wall with a doorway.

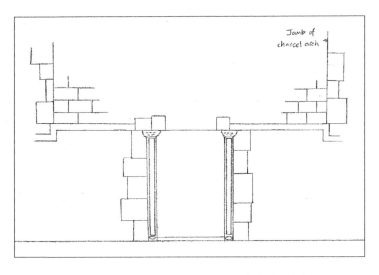

'Stone Screen between the nave and choir of the
Church of Grey Friars, Reading.'
Original by J. C. Buckler 1860
This drawing, by the author, omits the dimensions

This original east wall had two windows, one at the end of each of the aisles. John Billings wrote, in 1846:

> The aisles terminated with the nave, and were pierced with one east window in each; of what kind we can scarcely tell, one end being so completely covered with ivy, that it defies penetration, and the other bricked up, shews nothing but the mere outline of the window, which differs from the aisles inasmuch as it is longer and acutely pointed.[74]

Greyfriars as the Town Bridewell,
about 1775
by Samuel Hieronymous Grimm

This is the earliest drawing of the nave of the friary[75]

Before the Reformation, the only consecrated part of any English church was the quire.[76] It is interesting, therefore, that when the friary was dissolved in the 16th century it was the non-consecrated part of the church, the nave, that was given to the town as a Guildhall.

Opposite is a conjectural plan of the friary church, superimposed on a plan of the current church.[77] Although the restored church has transepts, it is not likely that the friary church had them. The original nave was most probably simply rectangular. Occasionally, however, a Franciscan church did have a transept in order to accommodate side chapels and it is known that the Reading friary did have at least one altar in the north-east of the nave.[78] During the restoration building works in 1862, evidence was found of ancient foundations that were believed to show the church originally did have a north transept. However, the remains could have been the foundations of the cloister wall, since the cloister would have been on the north side near that location.

The completed church had stained glass windows. The General Constitutions of the Franciscan Order of 1260 had stated that only images of Christ on the cross (the rood), St Francis and St Anthony of Padua were allowed in Franciscan church windows.[79] It was not very long, however, before other saints and stories were illustrated in them too. It is not known which images were in the Reading House windows. The only reference to them is at the dissolution, with the description of 'windows decked with grey friars'.[80]

The church was built in the architectural style now known as Decorated, or Decorated Gothic. This type of architecture flourished in England for a century from about 1280. The most noticeable aspect of this style, which can be seen in Greyfriars today, is the delicate and curved window tracery.

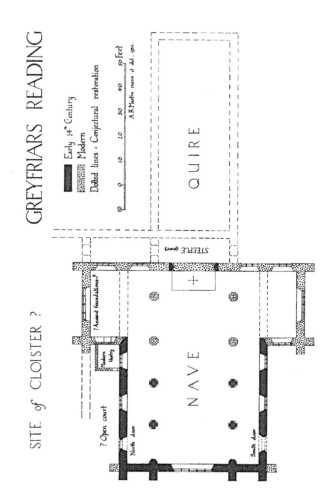

GREYFRIARS READING

SITE of CLOISTER ?

Early 14th Century
Modern
Dotted lines = Conjectural restoration

10   0   10   20   30   40   50 Feet

A.R. Martin mens. d del. 1921.

QUIRE

STEEPLE (site)

✚

NAVE

? Ancient foundations

Modern Vestry

? Open court

North door

South door

The west window is particularly notable. Pevsner's description is matter of fact: 'The large five-light west window has reticulated tracery'.[81] John Man, in his *History of Reading* of 1816, is more enthusiastic: 'The windows on the north and south sides were small, without any ornaments, but that at the west end is still admired, as a beautiful specimen of gothic architecture'.[82]

John Billings wrote in *The Archaeological Journal* in 1846 that 'the west window is by far the finest part of the whole edifice... The tracery is of a flowing character, simple but elegant.'[83]

External view of
Greyfriars Church West Window
showing its reticulated (net-like) tracery

Internal view of part of the west window
showing the ogee curves of the tracery

Near the top of the west window, but not visible from the ground, is a 14th century mason's mark, shown below.

The plan on page 39 shows in black where the stone in the church dates from the original late 13th/early 14th century. The north, west and south walls of the nave (not including the transepts) and the windows in them are original. On the west wall, at the ends of the arches, are four 14th century 'head-stops'. They are generally not in a good condition, although two of them remain recognisable as faces of friars, to judge from their hairstyles.

14th century head-stops on the west wall
Left: on the south
Right: on the north

The four windows in the aisles:

are of three lights, with segmental heads – the mouldings are remarkably plain – but in this style we frequently find very beautiful and sometimes intricate combinations of tracery, with but meagre and shallow mouldings – the heads are divided similarly to the west window, feathered and cusped. The label-mould to these windows, to the west window and to the arcades, is precisely the same in contour, differing only in size.[84]

The two pairs of columns nearest the west wall are made almost entirely of original stone, while the others are a mixture of original and nineteenth century stone. The arches throughout the church are original. John Billings wrote:

> The aisles are separated from the nave by a stone arcade of five compartments, the arch nearest the chancel of each arcade being narrower and more acutely pointed than the others. The mouldings of both pillars and arches are very well worked and in tolerable preservation.[85]

John Man gave the following description:

> The aisles are separated from the body of the church by lancet pointed arches, springing from six [there are 8] clustered stone columns, with circular capitals, extending on each side [of] the nave from the two extremities; the spaces between the pillars are each fourteen feet four inches, except the two at the east end, which are only eleven feet apart; but why these differ from the general plan cannot now be conjectured.[86]

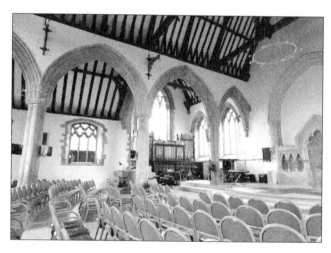

The narrower span of the arch that meets the east wall
(to the right) is clear from this photograph

The narrower span of the most easterly arches does indeed remain unexplained. One possibility is that these are narrower in order to carry the weight of the bell tower above them. In *Franciscan Architecture in England*, A. R. Martin, speaking not of Reading specifically but of the development of friaries over time, wrote:

> It was probably the increase in size of the steeple [in the late 13th century] which led to the introduction at first of one and later of two cross walls of masonry between the nave and the quire to carry the additional weight. With the introduction of the masonry steeple the two cross walls became essential, and as its height increased the two arches in these walls tended to become narrower.[87]

If this had been the case in Reading, that the bell tower was above the narrower arches, then the walking place would have been in the space between the last column and what is now the east wall. However, in the east wall, as it was before being rebuilt in 1862, there were windows at the end of the two aisles (see page 37). This wall would then have to be the west wall of the walking place as its east wall would have been shorter, of the same width as the quire.

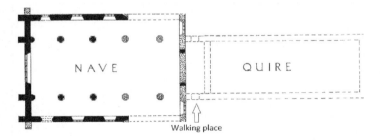

This plan shows the most likely layout of the friary church.
There was a tower with at least 2 bells
above the walking place

The length of the current church is 77 feet 6 inches (23.6m) and the whole width of the nave (not transepts) is 51 feet 6 inches (15.7m). The side aisles are 10 feet 6 inches (3.2m) wide. This compares, for example, with the dimensions of Reading Abbey's nave: 200 feet (61m) by 40 feet (12.2m).[88] The Abbey's nave, not including the aisles, was 5 times longer than its width. The friary nave, not including its aisles, was only 2½ times longer than its width.

The interior of the friary nave would have been a colourful place, mainly due to the stained glass windows mentioned above. There was also some painting on at least one of the walls. It was quite possible that most of the walls carried illustrations of Bible stories or paintings of saints. John Doran, in his 1835 *History of Reading*, wrote:

> On the wall (on each side of the arch which led into the choir), which had been whitewashed over, some remains of painting have been traced, but too much defaced to enable the subject to be understood.[89]

The wall paintings might have been illustrations from the Life of St Francis. The two favourite scenes depicted in Franciscan churches were Francis preaching to the birds and Francis receiving the stigmata. However, the late 13th century saw an increase in subjects taken from 'the Infancy and Passion of Our Lord, with scenes from the life of the Blessed Virgin, and from the lives of the saints, especially those saints who were popular at the time and whose miracles had a close connection with the needs and misfortunes of the people'.[90]

One other interesting part of the original building survived from the 14th century. In 1862, during the restoration of the church, a number of old floor tiles were found. The *Reading Mercury* reported:

> GREY FRIARS' CHURCH. – During this week a very curious piece of pavement has been dug up under the north doorway. It

consists of the ordinary small encaustic tile ornamented with figures of dogs, cats, stags and various other animals. It has been carefully preserved, with the view, we believe, of replacing it when the work is far enough completed for this purpose.[91]

Hare

Dog

Stag

Geometrical design

This small piece of paving, about a square yard in all, was all of the original paving that was found. At first the tiles were replaced on the floor by the font in the restored building,[92] but they are now in a framed display in the church, in the north-west corner, with this accompanying text:

Original Early XIV Century Paving Tiles made of red clay inlaid with white slip and glazed. The designs are neither heraldic nor religious, but show a hare upon a background of trefoil foliage, a dog with a collar and a bell upon a background of oak leaves and acorns, an antlered stag, and a geometrical design of four squares divided gyronwise.[93]

In 1846, sixteen years before the discovery of these tiles, John Billings had searched for the original flooring and wrote: 'No traces of the floor are visible, and, on digging, no remains of the pavement or tiles could be discovered; the floor probably was taken up when the church was converted into a bridewell, the nave being divided off into airing yards'.[94]

The walls of the church were built of flint with stone quoins, and plastered inside. John Man wrote that the 'structure was principally composed of flints, put together with so much precision as almost to appear one solid mass, and is, beyond a doubt, one of the completest works of the kind now existing'.[95] In a similar vein, John Billings wrote:

Externally the flint work was laid in regular courses, and the flints split and squared. The skill and management of the old builders, and the ease with which they made the most rugged materials bend to their purpose, was never better displayed than in the construction of these walls; the thin narrow joints, sharp surface, and beautiful appearance of the flint work, far surpasses the best attempts of modern days, and proves that what else the Church may have been, that it was at least the school of sound architects and good workmen.[96]

When the church was restored it was hoped that a chancel would be built at some point in the future. It could not be built at the time since the land belonged to Mr. Charles Andrewes JP and Town Councillor. His house was built on some of the area that would be needed for the chancel and had a servants' wing that actually abutted the church's east end wall.

When the east wall of the church was rebuilt in 1862, part of the wall was faced with brick and not with flint. The expectation was that, if and when the land could be bought by the church, the bricks would then be removed and the chancel built. However, even though the church has owned the property next door since 1884, no chancel was ever built.[97]

There were many burials in the friary over the three centuries of its life. In 1862-3, when the work of restoration was being carried out:

> The architect [Mr William Woodman] found, on excavating for the new building, the ground entirely occupied by human remains, interred not only in the church [i.e., the friary's nave] but in the ground adjoining it, and he found many vaults in Mr. Andrewes's garden, especially on the site of the chancel, which were carefully left untouched, no attempt being made to examine them. The chancel arch, and east wall of the nave were found in an unsafe condition from the wall having been built over a body, the skeleton of which was entire, and which had evidently been laid in the foundation as the wall was being built.[98]

There were also some human remains uncovered when the Vicarage was demolished and rebuilt in 1963. The report in the Berkshire Archaeological Journal states: 'Two extended human skeletons were discovered when workmen cut through some graves while digging the footings for the new Greyfriars Vicarage, on the west side'.[99]

When Greyfriars Church was being reordered in 2000 the entire church floor was excavated in order to lay a new system of underfloor heating. Beneath the east wall, just outside the line of the arches on the north, the upper part of a doorway was discovered. This door, entirely underground, was very likely to have led to one of the vaults mentioned in the newspaper report above, sited underneath either the nave or the quire floor. It may even have led to a crypt or undercroft and a series of vaults, as this is not unknown elsewhere.[100]

The newspaper report quoted above believed that the remains of the body under the east wall were deposited there before the wall was built. This was not necessarily the case, as there are examples of burials elsewhere in similar situations:

> So great was the number of people wishing to be buried in mendicant [friary] churches that tombs had to be tightly packed into side aisles, where every possible space was used. The space near walls was at times extensively undermined by the improper practice of constructing vaults for interment within the area of the walls, thereby weakening structure.[101]

It was a much sought after privilege to be buried, preferably in the habit of a friar, in the grounds of a friary. It was even better if the grave could be within the church, beneath the floor of the quire or in a monumental tomb in the nave and as near to the east end as possible.[102] It is not known if there were any tombs with effigies on top, whether of stone or of wood, inside the Reading friary church, but it is very likely.

The quire would have had an altar at its east end, dedicated to St Francis.[103] This high altar could not be used for 'private masses', that is for any mass that someone had paid for in memory of the dead. The Reading House had at least one other altar, on the north side of the nave,[104] for these masses to be said. There would have been one altar in the church dedicated to Mary, as 'all mendicant orders were enthusiastic advocates for the devotion and honouring of Mary as Queen of Heaven'.[105] Such altars would be in a side chapel, screened from the main body of the nave. There would also have been statues in the church, almost certainly of the Virgin Mary and of St Francis, but there may have been many more.

The friary would have had a dedication ceremony and a patron saint. Unfortunately we do not know when or to whom it was dedicated. Friary churches could be consecrated by any bishop, but there was generally a preference for a Franciscan. When the Franciscan bishop Peter of Bologna was in England from about 1320 to 1331 he was called upon to dedicate several friary churches, but unfortunately the names of the friaries were not recorded. It is possible that Reading was one.[106]

In 1726, the Franciscan historian Anthony Parkinson wrote of Reading that 'Here was a famous Convent of Franciscans... but [I] cannot learn who was the Founder here, what was the Title of the House, or that it had any endowments of lands', although elsewhere he calls it 'the Convent of St Francis, at Reading'.[107] Coates wrote in 1802 that 'the House is said to have been dedicated to St James',[108] but unfortunately he gave no information about who it was who had said this. Of the 60 Franciscan Houses in England and Wales, the dedication is known for 36 (that I can find), and 32 of them are to St Francis. The others are to St John the Baptist (at Exeter) and to St Mary (Salisbury, Stafford and not surprisingly at Walsingham).[109] Doran (in his *History of Reading* 1838) summed it up neatly by writing 'it is said, but not with certainty, to have been dedicated to St James'.[110] The likelihood is that the dedication was therefore to St Francis, but with a possibility that it was to St James. If it had been dedicated to St James, perhaps it was to reflect the saint's local popularity, since the abbey possessed the Hand of St James as one of its relics.[111]

Picture then the townspeople of Reading coming into the friary church sometime in the middle or late 14th century. As they entered the nave, they would see the side chapels, screened off but still visible, and perhaps linger by the tombs, also in the side aisles. They would take time to look at the painted scenes on the walls. They would bow in prayer before some statues (also painted). They would gasp at the colours of the stained glass windows as the sun streamed in through them. They would then stand to listen to one of the friars as he gave the sermon, and strain to hear the chanting friars from the quire, heard through the open doorways and across the corridor of the walking place. They would have to stand because the nave would have been empty of chairs – at least until the late middle ages, perhaps in the late 15th or early 16th century, when gradually seating began to be provided.

The Guildhall
Greyfriars, Chichester

This is the quire of the second friary
dating from the late 13th century

This building is not open to the public
but can be hired for weddings

Above: Cloister with frater (refectory) above
Dunwich, Suffolk

Below: Remains of the south-western corner of
the cloister buildings
Great Yarmouth, Norfolk

Chapter 5

The Franciscan Order in England

The Reading House of friars minor took its place in the wider organisation of the Franciscan Order. Following a papal decision in 1231, the friars were not subject to any diocesan authority and so they operated freely outside the organisation of the church.[112] Reading was within the Diocese of Salisbury throughout the life of the friary and, although the friary was not under the bishop's authority, it maintained strong links with him.

The Order of Friars Minor had two parallel strands of leadership, both men being chosen by the Pope. One took the role of guardian of the Order against other religious bodies whenever any disputes arose, and the other was in charge of the discipline and maintenance of the Order.

In the first strand, under the Pope, the leader of the Franciscans was the Cardinal Protector, who was the representative of the Order in the Papal Court. Under the Cardinal Protector, in each of the Provinces of the Order, there was a Preserver (or Conservator) of Privileges. We met examples of these in chapter 3, with Cardinal Mattheo Orsini being the Cardinal Protector and John Peckham, the Archbishop of Canterbury, being the Preserver of Privileges of the Friars Minor in the English Province.

The second strand was led by the Minister-General of the Order, whose authority was directly from the Pope, and who often resided in Rome to be near the centre of the church's decision making and power. Each of the Provinces had their own Minister-Provincial, and so since 'England' was one of these Provinces (although Houses in Wales and, at times,

Scotland were included for the period we are considering) the leader of the Franciscans in this country was the Minister-Provincial of England. This man divided his time between travelling around his Province and being a representative of the Province at General Chapters, chaired by the Minister-General.

The Province of England was separated into clusters of Houses, called Custodies, with each cluster being overseen by a *custos*, or custodian:

> The custodian held office for a number of years and his functions may be described as those of a localized provincial minister and permanent visitor... In every custody one convent had to be assigned for the reception and training of novices. In England the custody acquired a special importance as an educational area; each custody maintained a special school of theology.[113]

Initially there were eight Custodies, and from time to time there were changes for some Houses, which were moved from one Custody to another. However, for most of the life of the Reading friary, there were seven Custodies, with Reading always being within the Custody of Oxford.

The seven Custodies were:[114]

Custody:	Houses:
London	London, Salisbury, Canterbury, Winchester, Southampton, Lewes, Chichester, Winchelsea, Ware
Oxford	Oxford, Reading, Northampton, Bedford, Stamford, Nottingham, Leicester, Grantham, Aylesbury
Cambridge	Cambridge, Norwich, Bury St Edmunds, King's Lynn, Ipswich, Colchester, Yarmouth, Dunwich, Walsingham

York	York, Lincoln, Grimsby, Scarborough, Beverley, Doncaster, Boston
Bristol	Bristol, Hereford, Bridgwater, Exeter, Gloucester, Dorchester, Bodmin, Carmarthen, Cardiff
Worcester	Worcester, Coventry, Lichfield, Shrewsbury, Chester, Llanfaes, Bridgnorth, Stafford, Preston
Newcastle	Newcastle, Hartlepool, Carlisle, Roxburgh, Haddington, Durham, Richmond, Berwick, Dundee, Dumfries

Each year a Provincial Chapter was held in one of the larger Houses, presided over by the Minister-Provincial and attended by the *custos* of each Custody, the warden of each House (who was sometimes called a guardian) and an elected representative friar from each House. Every office holder formally resigned their office each year and the Chapter appointed officers for the next year. In practice, this was often re-electing the previous office holder, but replacements did occur. When this happened, the deposed office holder simply became an ordinary friar.[115]

Reading Abbey was of a suitable size to hold national ecclesiastical councils and even the parliament of the land in its chapter house, but the Reading friary was not large enough to hold the Provincial Chapter of its Order. Of the (mostly) annual Provincial Chapters from the 13th to the 16th century, the locations of 55 Chapters are known, in a total of 18 different Houses, with three quarters having taken place at London, Oxford or Cambridge, the largest three friaries in England.[116]

The number of friars at many of the Houses is not known. When the friaries were closed down under Henry VIII, mostly in 1538, the warden and friars signed the document of surrender and so, where this document survives, at least the final number of the friars at the House can be known. This, however, was in nearly all cases a lower number than the House would have accommodated in previous centuries. For example, Salisbury's document of surrender was signed by 10 friars, although the House was known to have had about 40 friars in 1290.[117]

Unlike monks in a monastery, who rarely if ever moved from place to place, friars were more mobile as they owed obedience directly to the Minister-General and so could be either directed, or allowed, to change location.[118] Giles Coventry, for example, who was one of the signatories to the Surrender of the Reading friary in 1538, had been warden of Walsingham friary in 1535.[119]

Of the 65 Franciscan friaries built in the English Province three were in Wales (Cardiff, Carmarthen and Llanfaes) and five in Scotland (Berwick, Dumfries, Dundee, Haddington and Roxburgh). There were three other Franciscan Houses built in Scotland – Lanark, Inverkeithing and Kirkcudbright – but these were never considered to be part of the English province as they were all founded after the Scottish Houses were separated from the English Province to become the Scottish 'vicariate' in 1329.[120]

All trace of most of the friaries has disappeared, with just 13 locations in England having significant remains left. Greyfriars in Reading has the distinction of being the only one still in use as a church. Much of the building dates from the late 13th/early 14th century, also making it one of the earliest of the Franciscan remains. Unsurprisingly, Greyfriars Church is a Grade I listed building.[121]

The other significant Franciscan friary remains can be seen at: Canterbury, Chichester, Coventry, Dunwich, Gloucester, Great Yarmouth, King's Lynn, Lincoln, Richmond (Yorkshire), Walsingham, Ware and Winchelsea.

Greyfriars Chapel
Canterbury

Greyfriars, Lincoln

The earliest parts of this building date from the middle of the
13th century, and so are older than Greyfriars Church, Reading.

This was probably the friary's church.
By 1300 it had been divided into two storeys
with a vaulted undercroft below.

The building is currently unused and rarely open to the public.

Chapter 6

Friary Life

The daily routine of life in the friary revolved, as at the abbey, around the divine office. The friars took their places in the quire to sing the services throughout the day and night. In the morning, the friars gathered in the chapter house where the warden conducted any general business and allocated duties to each friar for the day. Like all conversation between friars in the friary, the chapter was conducted in Latin.

The friars' daily tasks included a variety of domestic duties as well as the need to look after the friary's land and animals. One of the friars would be in charge of the instruction to be given to any novices. If there was a friar soon to go to university, then he would be set to study in preparation.

Important among the daily tasks, given that the friars lived on alms from the people, was that of begging for food. The warden decided who and how many should go out to the town, with the friars always sent in twos, sometimes with a lay assistant – a servant or a small boy – to carry the offerings, especially if these were in coins:[122]

> These Franciscans were, in a short Time, spread over the Christian World; possessing nothing but merely living by the Gospel; in Food and Rayment they manifested their voluntary Poverty; and going bare-foot, girt with a knotted Cord, gave the greatest example of Humility imaginable... they wholly lived on the Charity of others... going constantly by Couples with Wallets on their Shoulders to receive Alms.[123]

Although much of the friars' time was taken up with duties at the friary, their main work was 'not within the precinct but among the laity of whom they came, and in particular among the very poorest classes in the towns and the lepers who were entirely outside the sphere of any existing ecclesiastical influence'.[124]

Sunday services were held in the friary church to which many locals came. The friars sang the mass in the quire, while the locals stood to listen in the nave, with the walking place doors open between the two. One friar would then come to the nave to preach the sermon. Services would also be held on festival days and on rainy days when the people were encouraged to shelter in the church and the friars took the opportunity of preaching to them.

The naves of Franciscan churches were often wider and shorter than other contemporary churches, with the aim of making them more suitable for hearing the sermon, as:

> The Franciscans attached great importance to preaching. St Bernardino of Siena held attendance at sermons even more valuable than attendance at mass. 'If of these two things you can only do one – either hear the mass or hear the sermon – you should let the mass go rather than the sermon'. The friars, laying such stress on the sermon, seem to have allowed themselves considerable latitude in shortening the office, and the seculars complained at the Council of Lyons in 1274 that people preferred the short masses of the friars and neglected the ordinary services. It seems clear that church-going increased in the later Middle Ages, and it is reasonable to attribute the growth of this practice to the influence of the friars. [125]

Robert Grosseteste, who had been the first 'lecturer to the friars' at Oxford and had been consecrated as Bishop of Lincoln at Reading Abbey in 1235, wrote to Pope Gregory IX in 1238 that the friars minor:

> illuminate our whole country with the bright light of their preaching and teaching… If your Holiness could see with what

devotion and humility the people run to hear from them the word of life, to confess their sins, to be instructed in the rules of living, and what improvement the clergy and regulars have gained by imitating them, you would indeed say that 'upon them that dwell in the valley of the shadow of death hath the light shined'.[126]

Preaching did not only occur in the church. A friar, carrying a preaching cross (see the drawing below), would stand in any convenient spot where people could easily gather, and speak.

Friar with
preaching cross[127]

The friars' sermons were 'generally vivid, sometimes witty, and often very outspoken. The preachers not only expounded the Scriptures – sometimes with considerable flights of imagination – they denounced injustices and moral failings and gave their views on political and social issues...

With the sermons went pastoral care and counselling. The friars preached in such a way that a good many people wanted to consult them afterwards or to make their confessions'.[128]

One thing that did not accompany preaching was any collection of money. This was forbidden in the Statutes of the Franciscan Order.[129]

The attractiveness of the friars' services could be a problem for local parish clergy as it often resulted in a fall in the number attending the parish church. There was little that the parish clergy could do about it, as:

> The parochial clergy were, for the most part, incapable of doing much in the way of preaching. It was not generally regarded as very important and few of the clergy had any training for it.[130]

A second bone of contention between the clergy and the friars was that of hearing confessions, which the parish priest believed to be his prerogative. Not every friar was ordained a priest (although by the 14th century most were),[131] and not all the Order's priests were licensed to hear confessions. However, even in the small friaries, like at Reading, it was expected that there would be at least one friar licensed to hear confessions.

Parish clergy were against the friars hearing confessions because they believed that it undermined the connection between parish priest and parishioner. The parishioner, on the other hand, would be more likely to go to a friar since not only was it easier to confess to a stranger rather than the priest who knew them, but also the friars had the reputation of being more lenient than the parish priests in the penance given.[132]

The third area of conflict with the parish priest was that of burial rights – and as these involved fees, they tended to be the most serious objections. As we have seen, burial in the friary was a popular choice for those who could afford it, and for each time this happened a parish priest missed out on a much needed part of his income.

At first sight, this issue could have brought the Reading friary into conflict with the abbey as well, since the original agreement in 1233 was that only friars would be buried in the friary grounds unless a special licence had been granted by the abbot. The grant of 1285 was even more specific: 'They [the friars] have also promised that whatsoever liberty of sepulture they enjoy or shall hereafter enjoy, they shall never receive for burial in their cemetery or church or elsewhere the bodies of deceased parishioners of the monastery or of the churches appropriated to the abbot and convent in the town of Reading or outside without the special licence of the abbot and convent.' However, Pope Boniface VIII's Bull *Super Cathedram* in 1300 allowed friars the right to bury lay people in their precincts, and this would have superseded the abbey's injunction.[133]

In addition to burial fees, the friary became the beneficiary of many local people's wills, as can be seen from the records associated with the Reading House given in chapter 7 below. These were often linked with the institution of masses for the deceased, such as trentals (on the 30th day after death or burial) or annual masses. Parish priests were legally entitled to a quarter of the 'gifts, bequests and fees given by their parishioners to the friars', although there is no mention of whether this was ever enforced. In 1521 Pope Leo X exempted the friars from this payment.[134]

From the fifteenth century some friaries increased their income by allowing people to lodge within the friary in return for money or land. This allowance of shelter and support, followed in due time by burial within the friary, was known as a corrody. At the time of the dissolution in 1538, at the Reading friary there were 'three pretty lodgings', according to the report of Dr John London, Cromwell's agent, of which 'the warden keeps one, Mr Ogle the King's servant, another, and an old lady called my lady Seynt Jone the third'.[135] These three houses can be seen in the drawing of the friary in John Speed's map of Reading, shown on page 32.

Each Franciscan House had to have at least one qualified theologian who could give instruction to his fellow friars. For example, at the dissolution in 1538, the Reading friary had two of its number who were qualified as STB, standing for *Sacrae Theologiae Baccalaureus*, or Bachelor of Sacred Theology.

To receive the qualification of STB, or DD (Doctor of Divinity), a friar would be sent by his convent to one of the universities. From Reading that would probably mean going to Oxford. The convent would be committed to the financial support of the friar throughout his time studying. The course of study at the university lasted several years. If after six years of studying the bible the friar was found to have sufficient understanding and moral character, then he was admitted to 'oppose in theology' for the following two years. This required the friar to be able to dispute a defined range of topics, first as opponent and later as respondent.

After a total of about nine years of theological study, the friar, if successful, would first study and then lecture on the *Sentences* of Peter Lombard, a 12th century compilation of theology. For his examination, he then had to preach three sermons (at least one in Latin) and lecture on a book of the bible. At the end of his course he was examined separately by eight theologians.[136] He deserved his qualification after that!

Chapter 7

The History of the Reading House

The Reading friary was not an important House. Consequently it does not appear in many records, unlike its famous neighbour, the abbey, or its nearest Franciscan neighbour at Oxford. However, from the 14th to the 16th centuries, it steps out of the shadows occasionally, mostly in bequests in wills.

The first name that can be associated with the friary is Warner, who was warden in 1320. The *Sarum Episcopal Register* notes that Roger de Mortival, Bishop of Salisbury, licensed Warner to hear confessions in the Salisbury Diocese in that year.[137]

Shortly after this, in 1326, there is an entry in the *Queen's Remembrancer Wardrobe Accounts* that has been taken to imply that there were 26 friars at Reading at that time.[138] However, the number of friars is inferred from a calculation based on the cost of cloth for habits. Other indications of the number of friars do not go above 13, and so I believe that this reference actually means that each of the 13 friars received two habits (see page 18 for a similar occasion).

It is unfortunate that so little remains of the documentation from the Franciscan Provincial Chapters. One of the few pieces that does is a very incomplete list of friars who had died between pairs of Chapter meetings in the early 14th century. Each friary was required to send this information in accordance with the General Constitutions of 1260.

The document starts with noting that at the Provincial Chapter at Lincoln on 1 August 1327, Williamus de Assewell became the guardian, or warden, at Reading.

Five deaths at Reading were listed between that date and the next Provincial Chapter on 8 September 1328. The friars who had died at Reading were:[139]

Ricardus de Waneting, priest and teacher
J[ohannes] de Bokingham, priest and teacher
Johannes de Graue, priest and teacher
Willelmus de Abindon, teacher
Willelmus de Okam,[140] priest and teacher

It is surprising that there were five deaths out of a complement of thirteen friars in just over a year. Perhaps there was an epidemic in the town, although no record seems to have come down to us to suggest it, other than this one.

The document has the name of just one other Reading friar, that of Helias de Aylesbirye, priest and teacher, who probably died around 1333.

There is then a gap of about 40 years before the next reference to the Reading friary. This includes the dreadful period when the country was ravaged by the Black Death, which came to Reading, as everywhere in England, in the autumn of 1348, lasting until September of the following year. It came again at intervals over the next 30 years. Estimates vary, but it is thought that during 1348–9 up to 50% of the population of England died. The death toll among the grey friars was almost certainly much higher as they would have selflessly sought to care for the sick and dying. Possibly as many as two thirds of the grey friars in England died.[141] It took many years for friaries to recover. The population of the country did not reach its previous level until Elizabeth's reign, over 200 years later.

After the Black Death, the character of the Franciscan order in England was changed. Previously it had clung to the ideal of poverty and a mendicant life, not wishing even to handle coins let alone own property. Friaries became more likely to accept gifts of money in exchange for spiritual services, for example fees for masses said for the dead or money for a certain number of prayers to be said in the Chapel of St Francis.[142] Both Chaucer's *The Canterbury Tales* and Langland's *Piers the Plowman* were written after the Black Death of 1348–9 and their friars (although not necessarily Franciscans) bear little resemblance to the Franciscan ideal of a century earlier.

It might be thought that, with the Reading House being such a small foundation, the friary would have had a difficult time clinging on to its existence for the next few years after the Black Death. However, it seems that not only did it survive, but it gained its first renowned theologian: John Lathbury. The 18th century Franciscan historian, Anthony Parkinson, wrote of him:

> Br. John Lathbery, of the Franciscan Convent of Reading, in Berks, was a Doctor of Divinity of Oxford, and is greatly commended by Leland for his manifold Learning both sacred and Prophane; for he dived into the hidden Secrets of Natural Things, and was a finish'd Philosopher; he excell'd also in the Knowledge of Theological Learning. [143]

John Lathbury flourished in the middle years of the 14th century. He wrote many books, bequeathing several to the Reading friary. Lathbury 'died at Reading at an advanced age in 1362'.[144]

A 17th century writer, Brother Angelus of St Francis Mason, in his *Catalogue of English Franciscan Writers*, mentions some other books that were believed to be in the library of the Reading House from about the 1370s. As we shall see, they were not in the library at the dissolution in 1538, but no doubt they were in use there for many years. They were described by Parkinson:

> Br. Henry of Oxford was a Franciscan Doctor of Oxford; a Person greatly Experienced in all Learning, both Sacred and Prophane; of wonderful Piety also... He also was a famous Preacher; and in all Stations behaved himself as a Man of extraordinary Vertue, Learning, and Resolution, especially in the Pulpit, in his Sermons... To the lasting Memory of his Name, and the Improvement of Posterity, he publish'd One Book of *Sermons upon the Festivals*, another Book of *Sermons upon the Sundays*, and a Third Book of *Sermons upon the Week-days*; which said Works are said to have been kept in the Convent of St. Francis, at Reading, Berks, till the Dissolution of Religious Houses.[145]

In contrast to the library of four manuscripts that John Leland found when he visited the friary in the 1530s, it seems that in earlier years the friary had a large number of books. The 17th century antiquary, Anthony à Wood, wrote of this 'famous Convent of Franciscans' that it was 'furnish'd with a good Library'.[146] This should not come as a surprise since the Reading House had had such a learned man as John Lathbury living and studying there.

Meanwhile, the friary benefited from the generosity of the townspeople in their wills. In 1407 a baker in Reading Abbey and burgess of the town, John Cooper, left 3s 4d ($£^1/_6$) to the friars minor of Reading. His main bequest was to leave his house and garden to his wife Joanne. Of Cooper's religious bequests, the friars did well compared to the abbey, which received nothing, and Salisbury Cathedral, to which he gave 6d 'for the fabric'. Cooper wished to be buried in St Laurence's and so gave 5s to the vicar there, as well as 6s 8d to be distributed to the poor on the day of his burial.[147]

About 1413, William Boteler, or Butler, 'a Franciscan Doctor of Oxford and a Professor... very famous for piety and learning and... universally esteemed for his prudence, solid judgement and great worth', retired to the Reading friary, died and was buried there.

The most renowned Franciscan of his day, Boteler had been Minister-Provincial of England from 1408 to 1410. He wrote several learned books that were of great influence on the Church at the time, including *Against the English translation of the Scriptures*, which argued for burning all copies of the English translation of the Bible. His belief was that if the Scriptures were read by people who were not sufficiently qualified to understand them, it would 'be the Cause of infinite Errors, most foolish Interpretations, intolerable Abuses and grievous Scandals'.

He resigned his position as Minister-Provincial in 1410 and it was probably in that year that he retired to the Friary at Reading. Although there was a move to re-elect him as Minister-Provincial three years later, it is likely that he stayed in retirement and lived out his days quietly in Reading. [148]

Another of William Boteler's books, *De Indulgentiis Papalibus* or *Of Indulgences granted by the Pope*, was said to have been in the Reading friary library. [149]

On 25 May 1426 the splendidly named Parnell Baron made his will. Of his gifts to churches and churchmen, the abbey received 40s and the abbot 20s, St Mary's church 20s, and its vicar 40d. The friars also received 20s (£1), while Salisbury Cathedral was left 2d. Baron died in 1426, with probate of the will being granted on 2 December. [150]

Probably in the late 1440s, another former Minister-Provincial of England died and was buried at the Reading friary. He was Thomas Radnor, who was in post as Minister-Provincial in 1438. Before his election to that post he had become a Doctor of Divinity at Oxford and had resided at the Hereford friary. It is not known how long he had been at

Reading before his death, nor is the year of his death accurately known.[151]

John Hale, a carpenter and burgess of the town, had his last will and testament written on 3 September 1461. Two of his bequests are very interesting, as they are contributions towards the repair of the roads to Pangbourne (20s) and to Earlfield, or Earley Field (13s 4d). Apart from his property, which was to go to his wife Custancia (Constance), his largest bequest was for 33s 4d, cancelling most of what he was owed by St Laurence's church for their new church bells. Having left Salisbury Cathedral 2d and the abbey nothing, he bequeathed 3s 4d to the friars. Hale died soon after, as his will was proved in the following January.[152]

In 1475 Edward Blande, rector of St Mary's church, Burghfield, left legacies to several parish churches – possibly those he had been attached to in his parochial career, as none are in Reading – and 6s 8d to the friars minor of Reading. Blande appointed as his executor abbot John Thorne (the first of the two abbots of that name), in spite of not leaving either him or the abbey any bequest.[153]

John Leche, who is perhaps better known as John A'Larder from his role as steward to the abbot of Reading Abbey, in a will dated 10 June 1477 left a large bequest of £10 5s 3d to the friary. Leche died soon after, as the will was proved 5 weeks later on 14 July.[154] John A'Larder's name lived on in Reading through his endowment of eight almshouses in front of St Mary's Church in Old Street (now St Mary's Butts). These houses were demolished by the Corporation in 1886, opening up the view of St Mary's and enabling the widening of the road. The John A'Larder almshouses became part of the new Almshouses on Castle Street.[155]

Although the Franciscan Order was not under the authority of the episcopal church, a friar could only be ordained to the priesthood by a bishop (or of course by any higher rank of clergy). Not all friars became priests, but the Order needed a sufficient number to lead their Houses and to teach and hear confessions. On Ember Saturday (19 December) 1489, Reading friar William Wursley was ordained deacon by the Bishop of Salisbury, Thomas Langton, in Ramsbury church.[156]

Ramsbury, in Wiltshire just over the Berkshire border from Hungerford, is about 30 miles west of Reading. In the 10th century it had been the seat of a bishop, but the see was translated to Salisbury in 1075. Thomas Langton had been chaplain to Edward IV and appointed Bishop of Salisbury by Richard III in 1485. Surprisingly, he retained royal favour following the change of regime after the Battle of Bosworth. King Henry VII promoted him to be Bishop of Winchester in 1493. Eight years later Langton was selected to be Archbishop of Canterbury, but died of the plague before he could be confirmed in that office.

In 1491, the will of Thomas Beke of Reading left 20s to the friary, and his body for burial there. His burial within the friary precinct is therefore the earliest we know for certain of one who was not a friar.[157] Thomas Beke had been a very prominent man in the town for over 40 years, serving as member of parliament three times: in the parliaments of Henry VI in 1450–1, and of Edward IV in 1461–2 and 1478. Beke was also chosen as mayor of Reading twice, for 1458–9 and for 1462–3.[158]

Friar William Wursley, mentioned above, may be the same person as 'Brother William, Warden of the Friars Minor in Reading', who is the author of a letter now held in Berkshire Record Office.[159] The letter dates from 1492 and is written in Latin. In translation (by A.L. Humphreys) it says:

To his dearly beloved in Christ, Katherine Goddarde and William, her son, Brother William, warden of the Friars Minors in Reading, sendeth greeting and peace everlasting in the Lord. Considering and accepting with sincere esteem and affection your devotion, and of reverence for God to our Order, and desiring to reciprocate it in a way that shall be to your spiritual advantage, by tenor of these presents I receive you into the suffrages of our Order, both while you live and after your death, granting you full participation with us in all masses, prayers, preachings, vigils, labours, fastings, and other good works, which by God's mercy shall be done by the brethren committed to my care, adding further as a special grace, that when we have information of your deaths and this our present letter is produced to us, all shall be done for you that is customary to do for one of our own brethren deceased. Fare ye well and prosper in our Lord Jesus Christ and his Mother, the glorious Virgin. Given at Reading, in the year of our Lord 1492.[160]

Katherine Goddarde lived in Bucklebury, a village just over ten miles west of Reading. This letter assured both her and her son William of the friars' prayers ('suffrages') during their lives and of funeral rites as if they were members of the friary. Unfortunately, it does not specify the amount that Katherine gave ('these presents') to the friary for these benefits. It is interesting that Brother William said that Katherine and William would share the heavenly credit, as it were, for all that the friars accomplished as if they were present at all the services in the friary and partakers themselves in all the friars' other good works.

In carrying out 'all... that is customary to do for one of our own brethren deceased', it is likely that burial in the friary is implied. This, as has been said previously, was a much sought after final resting place and, together with a share in the good works of the friary, the beneficiaries would hope that their time in purgatory would be shortened considerably as a result.

This type of document is known as a 'letter of confraternity':

These 'letters of confraternity', as they were called, or certificates, were sold by the Minorites and other friars and entitled a deceased person to the prayers of the brethren. It was asserted that bundles of these documents were shamelessly carried about and sold to anyone willing to find the purchase money, the name of the purchaser being filled in at the time. In two instances, however, the only ones noticed by the editor of the second volume of *Monumenta Franciscana*, they were evidently specially written on behalf of the individuals named.[161]

This example adds a third occasion where the letter has not simply had a name added but has been specifically written to the individual named.

In what became the final 50 years of the friary's existence, wills dominate the documentary record. On 12 November 1493, Henry Kelsall, a clothier and landowner as far afield as Southampton and the Isle of Wight, shared out his considerable wealth in detail in his last will and testament. Kelsall, who had become a burgess of Reading in 1475, had been one of the two members of parliament for Reading elected for the only such gathering in the reign of Richard III, in January and February 1484.[162]

In a phrase reminiscent of the 14th century Latin *operi fratrum minorum* of Alan of Banbury's will (see page 30) that gave rise to the belief that 1311 was the date for the completion of Greyfriars church, Kelsall made several donations with the words 'I bequeth to the operacions of the chirch of...' The three ancient parish churches of Reading and the friary were each given 20s, Salisbury cathedral 12d, or 1s, and the abbey was not mentioned.

As well as remembering a great many of his wider family and his friends, Kelsall bequeathed money to 30 parish churches around Reading. He gave to each of the John A'Larder almshouses a bedspread and pair of sheets, allowing 4s per house. He also bequeathed money for the repair of six roads out from Reading, to 'Thele... Pangbo'ne... Shipping Mill... Burghfield Brigge... Canruende... and the way called the Ort lane'. [163] Kelsall also bequeathed money for a new tenor bell for St Laurence's church. This 'great bell' was installed and consecrated in 1498, and named after him as the 'Harry Bell'.[164]

On 10 April 1498 William Hether bequeathed his parish church, St Mary, 40s and to St Laurence, St Giles and the friary 6s 8d each. Hether left 12d to the 'mother cathedral of Salisbury', but nothing to Reading Abbey.[165] This will and the previous one are good examples of how the people of Reading considered the friary to be like one of the three ancient parishes, and not like the abbey, at least as regards their need for money.

The next will is that of Margaret Twyniho, or sometimes Twyneo or Twynhoo or Twinyhoo. She was born in Bradfield as Margaret Langford. Her first husband, Nicholas Carewe, was Lord of the Manor of Purley Magna until his death in 1458.[166] Margaret then married a man called Carant, and after his death she married William Twyniho. Margaret and William are named as the patrons of Sulham Church in documents in the late 1480s.[167] William Twyniho was appointed seneschal of all the bishop of Salisbury's lands in Dorset in 1491, which brought him the annual sum of £5.[168]

Margaret was widowed a third time and in July 1500 wrote her will.[169] This will is remarkable for the number of times the Reading friary is mentioned. After entrusting her 'sinfull soule unto almyghti god' she willed her body to be buried 'in the Church of the grey ffreres in Redyng in the chapel of blessid Saint Ffraunces', as near to the tomb where she had buried her father and mother as could conveniently be arranged. The chapel of St Francis was the quire, where the main altar, as in all Franciscan friaries, was dedicated to St Francis.

Margaret also gave the friary £25 for prayers to be offered there for herself 'and my frendes'. She further willed, although not with great clarity:

that another wele disposed prest be persuened to singe for me
and my frendis at saint Frances unto whom the Gray Freres by
the space of v years immediately after my deth the same prest to
have for his salere by the yer x marc and fynde him his wyne
and wages…

This bequest granted an annual fee of 10 marks (£6 13s 4d)
for 5 years for a 'well disposed priest' to sing masses at the
friary in memory of Margaret and her (unnamed) friends. The
frequency is not mentioned, but may have been weekly.

In addition, Margaret asked for something that, if it was
done, shows that the rule about private masses not being said
at the main altar in a friary no longer held:

I will that myn executors after the xij month of mynde doom do
ordeyne my dirge and masse to be said for me quarterly in the
chancel of saint Fraunces by the space of v yeare and to bestowe
at every dirge xx d.

Margaret's will was proved at Lambeth on 3 March 1501,
so she had died by then. There is an interesting possible sequel
to the story of Margaret's burial in the quire related in Charles
Coates' *History of Reading* of 1802:[170]

If this chapel of St. Francis was the Eastern chapel beyond the
choir, it seems very probable that the coffin and bones of
Margaret Twyniho were found in 1728, according to the
following account.

Coates then quotes a letter to John Loveday, not saying
who the author was. Unfortunately the events were not
reported in the contemporary *Reading Mercury*. Coates
quoted:

On Thursday Oct. 17, 1728, in the evening, was found in Mr. Heycock's fryars, about a yard from the middle of the foundation of the East end of the Bridewell, and scarce a yard under ground, a coffin of Freestone, six feet eight inches long from the outside to the outside, the stone being two inches and a quarter thick; it is likewise two feet three inches over, in the widest part, which is at the head; one foot five inches at the feet, and it is one foot two inches deep on the outside. The bones, which are but small, are thought to be a woman's, and are in it, and not quite rotten. It appears to have had no lid to it; but they found abundance of tiles before they came to it, which makes me think it was arched over with tiles.

'Heycock's fryars' was the name given to the land around the remains of the friary in the 18th century, from the east side around to the north. It was named after its owner, Joseph Heycock or Haycock, an apothecary, who had purchased the land in 1722. The land remained in the Heycock family until purchased by Lancelot Austwick in 1805.[171]

The nave of the friary church had become a Bridewell, or prison, by this time and the quire had long since been removed. The distance described, 'about a yard from the middle of the foundation of the East end of the Bridewell', if correct, would put the burial in the walking place between the nave and the quire.

Of course, there is no certainty that this body was that of Margaret Twyniho. Not only do we know from her will that Margaret's mother was buried near her, but we know from other sources that other women were buried in the friary too. Katherine Goddarde would have been buried there, according to the letter quoted above. There was also Edyth Chestre, 'wydowe of Redinge', who by her will of 24 January 1533 was to be buried in 'church of the ffreer minors there'.[172] It is very likely there were many other women buried in the friary, whether in the nave, the quire, or elsewhere.

The best we can say is that it is possible that the coffin found in 1728 contained the remains of Margaret Twyniho. Coates does not mention what was then done with the coffin and bones, but it was probably re-buried near where it was found. It may even have been one of the finds described above in either 1862–63, or 1963 (see page 48).

The next three references to the friary are from wills where the testator granted money in exchange for prayers for his soul to be said by the friars. In 1503 John Love, a draper, bequeathed 10s; John Wilcox, who had been mayor of Reading in 1500–1, left 3s 4d in 1506; two years later Christian Nicholas willed the friars 6s 8d.[173] Christian Nicholas had been MP for Reading in Henry VII's last parliament in 1504, and mayor of Reading for four years from 1491 to 1495, then again in 1497–8, 1499–1500 and finally 1507–8. He was mayor for four successive years because of a long running dispute between the abbot and the Guild Merchant of the town, which resulted in abbot John Thorne II refusing to choose a mayor for the three years from 1492 to 1495.[174]

On 4 March 1514, about a month before he died, Sir Thomas Englefield of Englefield House wrote his last will and testament. He had been a member of parliament, although not for Reading, and Speaker of the House for two parliaments. He had been appointed a King's Councillor in 1509, and was one of the executors of Henry VII's will.

In his own will, Englefield gave his executors discretion over where he was to be buried, giving instructions about a whole series of masses on specific holy days. He then continued:

> ...and I will myn executors cause me to have a dirige and a
> masse of Requiem in the Grey fryers at Redyng the day of my
> burying and they to have for the same vi s viij d and also I will
> that they have ij yeres thenne next folowing xl s a yere to pray

for my soulle in forme as folowith if it soo lyke them that is to say to sing v diriges yerly and v masses in forme folowing that is to say a masse of *Nos autem gloriari* and that to be sung the day of the exaltation of the Crosse, a masse of Jesu and that to be done the vij th day of august a masse of the assumption of oure Lady a masse of the Nativite of our Lorde and that to be doon uppon Cristmasse day a masse of the v wounds of our Lorde and that to be doon sunn day in palme son woeke...[175]

In May 1516 John Stanshawe made his will. He gave his body 'to be buried in the chapel of saint ffraunces within the church of the freres minors in Redyng'. He also bequeathed the friary 20s (£1) for the friars to pray for him after his death and 12d for the maintenance of the light before the rood in the 'chapell standing in the north side'. Then, for the first time, personal bequests to friars were made. Stanshawe left 6s 8d to 'frere John Thacham', the warden of the friary. He gave 12d to each of the friars who were priests and 4d to each of those who were not. Two friars were named among Stanshawe's five executors: John Thacham, the warden, and brother Henry Aleyn, Stanshawe's confessor.[176]

As will be described below, in 1540 after the suppression of the friary, all the friary land and buildings except the nave of the church were acquired by John Stanshawe's son, Robert.

On 20 July 1518 William Barker made his testament, saying:

I bequeath and comende my soule unto almighty god my creator and saviour to his blessed moder our Lady saynt mary and to all the hooly company of heven And my body to be buried in the church of the ffreres mynour in Readyng[177]

In the following year Robert Bryll, yeoman, bequeathed 10s to the friary to pray for his soul.[178]

The next record that mentions the friary is from 1521: the will of another former mayor and member of parliament for

Reading, William Justice. Having spent the first part of his life as a merchant in Southampton, rising through various civic offices to the status of mayor of that town in 1501–2, Justice moved to Reading by 1509. He was chosen as one of the town's MPs for the first of Henry VIII's parliaments, which met in January 1510. He was chosen again as MP for the second of Henry VIII's parliaments, which met intermittently from 1512 to 1514.[179]

At Michaelmas 1512 William Justice was selected as Reading's mayor by abbot John Thorne II of Reading Abbey from the three candidates put forward by the burgesses of the town. He was chosen as mayor a second time, serving from January 1517 to September that year, after Thomas Bye died in office.[180]

In February 1521, William Justice made his (very long and detailed) will 'within [his] dwellinge house in Redynge'. Having settled several bequests on the church of St Mary's, he then gave the other parish churches, of St Laurence and St Giles, 20s (£1) each, and then to the 'freres of the same [town]' 20s also. In addition, Justice bequeathed a little over £10 to pay for the tiling and repairing of the friars' 'house'.[181]

In the following month, William Trewe of St Laurence's parish made his more modest will. Unusually, rather than money, he gave to the 'friere [friary] in Reading' a quantity of 'whete' (wheat).[182]

Most of the people making their wills at this time are quite definite about where they wish their bodies to be buried. On 16 October 1527, Nicolas Hyde planned differently. That day, he wrote in his will: 'my body to be buried in that parish churche that it shall please god to call me out of this worlde'. In rather more usual fashion, he bequeathed 3s 4d to the 'convent of freres'.[183] Nicolas Hyde, a mercer, had been chosen to be mayor of Reading in September 1522. During his mayoral year, he was also selected to be one of Reading's MPs, attending Henry VIII's fourth parliament in the summer of 1523.[184]

There is an entry in the St Laurence's church inventories for 1531–2 that has an account for the cost of repairing the binding of the 'church books'. In the accounts mention is made of 'ffrere Peter', who is almost certainly the warden of the friary at this time, Peter Schefford (also known as Peter Lawrence). The 46s 8d ($£2^1/_3$) Brother Peter received was for the relatively rare skill of writing. It is interesting to note that this work was not carried out by the vicar of St Laurence's, Richard Bedowe.

Part of the account is shown below:[185]

Payd for iij buk skynes ij stag skynes & viij shepe skynes	xviij[s]	vj[d]
Payd for xxi rede skynes	vij [s]	
Payd for glew		xij [d]
Payd for small threde & pak threde	ij [s]	ij [d]
Payd for xv vellam skynes	x[s]	
Payd to the boke binder for byndyng of the bokes	xxiiij[s]	
Payd to ffrere Peter for wryttyng & notyng the new grayle & for the Vellam therto	xlvj [s]	viij [d]

Not long after this, Peter Schefford was one of three witnesses to Richard Bedowe's will, dated 15 November 1533 and proved at Lambeth on the following 21 January. Among the various bequests, Bedowe did not forget the friary: 'I bequeath to the freers mynours in Reading aforsaid xl s'.[186]

In July 1534 the son of Sir Thomas Englefield Snr. (see page 77) and successor to the Englefield estate, Sir Thomas Englefield Jun., wrote his will. The friary was, as in his father's will, the only church in Reading to receive any bequest:

I will there be iiij severall diriges and iiij severall masses be solemnly sung within the grey ffreres of Reding for my soule and for their payn I give to them xl s to be distributed amongst the convent in meate and drinke and other necessaries as the convent will appoint, and the warden not to medle therewith'.[187]

In July 1535, former mayor of Reading William Watts made his will.[188] He bequeathed to the friary and to each of the three churches of Reading 6s 8d, although St Laurence's received several other bequests, as befitted his home parish.[189]

In an undated will which was proved on 21 November 1537, Alys Adams bequeathed:

To the Gray Freres of Reding, xl *d.*
To every frere there that is a preest dwelling in Reding, xij *d.* To the Warden of the Gray Freres of Reding [Peter Schefford] my cupp fashioned like a pere with the cover... To the convent of Reding at my month mynde. xl *d*, and to every frere preest dwelling there, viij *d*, and to every young frere, iiij *d*, and to every boye, ij *d*...[190]

This, the last of the wills before the dissolution, has the greatest number of personal gifts to members of the friary, showing that the friary had come a long way from the original vow of poverty in the 13th century.

John Leland visited the Reading House in the 1530s and listed the books he found to be in the friary's library. Leland was made Keeper of Henry VIII's Libraries in 1530 and from 1533 he travelled around the country, while the monasteries were being suppressed, inspecting their libraries and adding to the King's Libraries from their contents. During his travels, from 1533 to 1536, he kept thorough notes of all he found. This manuscript was published in six volumes from 1715 by Thomas Hearne.

At the Reading friary, Leland found just four manuscripts. He noted:

Radingia apud Franciscanos:
 Beda de naturis bestiarum
 Alexander Necham super Marcianum Capellam
 Alexandri Necham Mythologicon
 Joannis Waleys commentarii super Mythologicon
 Fulgentii.[191]

That is:
Reading at the House of the Franciscans:
 Bestiary by Bede
 On Martianus Capella by Alexander Neckam
 Mythologicon by Alexander Neckam
 Commentary on the Mythologicon of Fulgentius by John
 Wallensis

The Venerable Bede (673–735) wrote many books in addition to the *Ecclesiastical History* he is most famous for, covering a wide variety of subjects from commentaries on bible books to a discussion of the composition of Latin verse. Bestiaries were popular in medieval times, being books of natural history, usually coupled with a moral lesson or biblical image. Bede's *Bestiary* does not seem to have survived, as I can find no reference to an extant copy, although there is a possibility in the Bodleian Library in Oxford, but its attribution to Bede is categorised as 'dubious'.

Alexander Neckam, born in St Albans in 1157, was a leading theologian of his time. Only two copies of his book *On Martianus Capella* survive, one at the Bodleian Library, Oxford, and the other at Trinity College, Cambridge. Neckam's book is not a religious work, but a commentary on the fifth century author Martianus Capella's *De nuptiis Philologiae et Mercurii*, an allegory which explores the 'seven liberal arts'.

The third and fourth books have *Mythologicon* in their titles. This was a compilation of classical myths and legends, each usually with a somewhat fanciful allegorical interpretation. Neckam's *Mythologicon* is unfortunately not known elsewhere, and no manuscripts survive.

The author of the fourth book, John Wallensis, was a renowned 13th century Franciscan who taught in Oxford and Paris. Fulgentius was a 5th century writer whose *Mythologicon* was very popular in medieval times. Wallensis's commentary may still exist. There are two manuscripts of commentaries upon Fulgentius, both bound up with other works by Wallensis, but as they are anonymous the attribution is not certain.[192]

Most of the Libraries described by Leland had many more manuscripts than this, but Franciscan Houses were not rich foundations. In Leland's lists there are several others that have just a handful of manuscripts, like Reading. However, as we have seen above, many books were at one time or another in the Reading friary's library. It is of course entirely possible that the friars at Reading had foreseen the likelihood of their library being ransacked and so had removed, and probably sold, most of their books before Leland's visit. This is what seems to have happened at Oxford, where instead of a well stocked library Leland found 'cobwebs in the library, and moths and bookworms... nothing, if you have regard for learned books'.[193]

In April 1536 the friary's warden, Peter Schefford, tried to recover money that the friary was owed for having said various masses requested by Arthur Plantagenet, 1st Lord Lisle, uncle to the king, Henry VIII. The warden wrote to Lisle's agent, John Husee, 'at the Lyon in Southwark, beyond London Bridge'.[194] Attempting to sweeten his message, Schefford sent Husee a pair of Reading knives as a token of his goodwill, and offered him 'a bed at the Friars when he comes into these parts'. The warden then detailed the reasons for his letter: there were two sets of masses that had been requested, and neither had been paid for.

The friary had said the masses for Lord Dudley, who had been Lord Lisle's wife Elizabeth's first husband. Dudley had been executed at the command of the king in 1510. In a trusting gesture, Schefford had sent the certificate confirming that the masses had been said to Husee via a certain Thomas Meryzth, a merchant, but the friary had not yet received 'the reward'.

Concerning the other masses that had been requested, the warden was adamant that no certificate would be forthcoming before payment. Schefford requested that Husee pay the money to the bearer of the letter, and then in due course the friary would issue Lord Lisle with the relevant certificate.

The dispute between these two parties continued. Although it may relate to a later set of masses, a year later Husee wrote to Lord Lisle that, although the warden of the grey friars at Reading had not yet sent the certificate for 'the other half of the masses', Husee had no doubt that it would arrive soon.[195] However, a fortnight later, Husee wrote to Lord Lisle, passing on a letter from the warden, in which the latter again refused to hand over the certificate without payment.[196]

No further letters exist between the friars and Lord Lisle, and so it must remain uncertain whether the long-running dispute was resolved before events overtook them...

Warden's seal, Reading Grey Friars,
on the Document of Surrender 1538

Pointed oval, about 2" by 1½"

The Annunciation

Author's drawing
from a drawing by B. Howlett
held in the British Library[197]

Conventual seal of Reading Grey Friars
on the Document of Surrender 1538

Pointed oval, about 1½" by 1"

Author's drawing
from a drawing by B. Howlett
held in the British Library[198]

Chapter 8

Dissolution in September 1538

By mid-September 1538 the life of the Reading friary was extinguished, the friars expelled and the church defaced and despoiled. The story of its demise is a small part of the much larger history of the death of the whole monastic movement in England, affecting hundreds of religious foundations and thousands of monks and friars.

The end result is straightforward to describe, although why Henry VIII did it and how he persuaded the country to acquiesce to it is not so straightforward to explain. His main objectives were to remove opposition to his divorce from his first wife Catherine and the subsequent arrogation of his position as Head of the Church in England, and to fill his empty coffers with all the wealth both in land and in moveable goods that he could lay his hands on.

The roots of the suppression of the monasteries went deep. The first royal action against any religious houses had taken place three hundred years before Henry VIII when King John seized the revenues of what were known as alien priories.

Alien priories, of which there were about 150, were generally Norman foundations that had been made dependent upon a foreign mother house. The daughter house sent its revenues abroad to support the parent foundation, and received both monks and the appointments of superiors in return.

Many Cluniac foundations were alien priories, placed under the authority of the Abbey of Cluny when they were established. However, although Reading Abbey was a

Cluniac foundation, it was not an alien priory as it was never under the Abbey of Cluny's authority, nor did it surrender its incomes to it.[199]

Most kings after John at one time or another appropriated the alien priories' revenues when in great need. Edward I not only did so at the start of his war with France in 1294, but also caused all alien priories within 20 miles of the coast to move inland as he believed them to be full of potential French spies.

In 1337 Edward III was in great need of money for his French wars. He borrowed items worth over £200 from Reading Abbey: two golden chalices, a golden paten, and a golden reliquary encrusted with sapphires, oriental pearls, rubies and other stones. Perhaps unsurprisingly, 'at the time of the loan [Edward III] promised either to return or pay for them, but there is no record of the fulfilment of the promise'.[200]

The king also seized the alien priories in the same year, keeping their revenues for the royal treasury for the next 23 years. He restored the priories in 1361, only to take them again eight years later.

By this repeated intrusion, alien priories had their revenues and sometimes their assets confiscated but the houses themselves were not closed down. However, that changed in the late 14th century. The alien priories were so often in the hands of the king that foreign abbeys gained little profit from them and so they began to look for opportunities to sell the priories off. About 1390, William of Wykeham, who among other appointments was Bishop of Winchester and Chancellor of England, obtained the pope's agreement to the purchase of the alien priories of Hornchurch and Writtle in Essex for his foundation of New College at Oxford.

In 1405, in response to Henry IV's need for finance, parliament suggested looking to fill his treasury from the goods of churchmen. This began a process that culminated in 1414, in the reign of Henry V. In a move that foreshadowed the later Henry's actions, Henry V dissolved all 140 alien priories then in existence and their estates were vested in the crown.[201]

In the late 15th century several religious houses were closed and their estates used for other purposes, but the closure in each case was due to the very small number of remaining personnel, sometimes even none at all. For example, in 1485 William Waynflete, Bishop of Winchester, gained the estates of the Augustinian priory at Selborne to add to his foundation at Magdalen College, Oxford, since the priory had been abandoned by its canons. In 1494, the houses at Mottisfont and Luffield were suppressed, with only three canons at the former and a prior and two monks at the latter. The profit from the estates was added to Henry VII's hospital at Windsor.

The process for each of these closures included seeking the permission of the pope. This was an important step since, regardless of the affiliation of the house, it was under papal authority. The pope's agreement was not always easy to obtain, and could be delayed a considerable time. In the example of the Augustinian priory at Selborne given above, Bishop Waynflete had taken the step of purchasing the estate in August 1485, before hearing from the pope that he had the pope's permission to do so. In fact since the pope's bull was dated 8 July 1486 and Waynflete died just over a month later on 11 August, the permission may not actually have reached him in his lifetime.

As we come to the reign of Henry VIII, the tone of the story changes. That change began not with the king, but with his Chancellor, Thomas Wolsey. An ambitious man, Wolsey sought honours and power wherever he could find it. By 1515 he was Archbishop of York, Lord Chancellor of England and a Cardinal, and in 1518 he became papal Legate. Pope Leo X also empowered Wolsey to 'visit' all the monasteries, priories and friaries in England, an inspection role that he wasted no time in putting into practice.

Cardinal Wolsey decided that he wanted to found a college in Oxford, and had chosen the Priory of St Frideswide, a House of Augustinian Canons, as his preferred location. At his visitation in 1520, the priory was in good condition and well run. Nevertheless, Wolsey petitioned the pope, Clement VII, to suppress the priory so that he could build his college. After much pressing, Clement granted the bull in April 1524, and the priory was closed down.

Wolsey followed this success up in 1528 by urging the pope to grant him the right to suppress other monasteries in order to found a school in Ipswich. Wolsey's messengers to the pope invented stories of lax morals at the monasteries, which persuaded Clement VII to agree to the dissolutions.

Wolsey's fall from power and subsequent impeachment brought an end to his suppressions of religious houses. Among the 44 articles of impeachment are the charges:

Also the said Cardinal hath not only, by his untrue suggestion to the Pope, shamefully slandered many good religious houses and good virtuous men dwelling in them, but also suppressed, by reason thereof, above thirty houses of religion. And where, by the authority of his bull, he should not suppress any house that had more men of religion in number above the number of six or seven, he hath suppressed divers houses that had above the number, and thereupon hath caused divers offices to be found by verdict, untruly, that the religious persons so suppressed had voluntarily forsaken their said houses, which was untrue, and so hath caused open perjury to be committed, to the high displeasure of Almighty God.[202]

Before long, Henry himself would be guilty of exactly these offences.

Following his decision that he wanted to divorce Catherine of Aragon so that he could marry Anne Boleyn, Henry petitioned the pope from 1527. The resulting lack of success spurred Henry onto the path that led to the break with the papacy and, through the 'Reformation Parliament', the Act of Supremacy in 1534. Among the provisions of this Act, which cut England off from the jurisdiction of Rome, was the transfer of papal authority over the religious houses to the crown of England.

This was followed by the requirement for all to take an oath declaring that Henry was supreme in the realm in all things spiritual and ecclesiastical. In April 1534, Henry sent two 'grand visitors' to administer the Oath to the various orders of friars, who were seen as the potentially troublesome ones among the religious orders.[203]

The first to fall foul of Henry's requirements were the Friars Observant, a reformed Franciscan movement. The Observants were created following the papal decree in 1322 which rescinded the Rule of Poverty for Franciscans, allowing them corporately to own property (see page 5). The non-Observant Franciscans, such as the House at Reading, came to be known as Conventual Franciscans to distinguish them from the Observants. It was not until 1480 that the Observants gained their first house in England, founded by Edward IV at Greenwich. Henry VII then built Observant Houses at Richmond (Surrey) and Newark, and caused the Conventual Houses at Canterbury, Southampton and Newcastle to be given over to the Observants. [204]

In 1534, the Observants not only refused to take the Oath of Supremacy, but also preached against Henry's marriage to Anne and his status as spiritual head of the church in England. Before long, the king suppressed the whole Observant order, handing their houses to the Augustinian or Austin friars, who had shown Henry loyal support. Over 200 Observant friars, which given that there were just six houses must have been most of them, were imprisoned. Fifty of them died there; the rest by permission of Thomas Cromwell were allowed to leave the country, for Ireland, France or Scotland.[205]

Throughout 1535 and 1536, Cromwell sent a small team throughout the land on the 'Visitation of the Monasteries'. By this Cromwell was able to gain much information about the houses, and also to disrupt their lives by various means. One particularly unsettling measure was that all religious persons under the age of 24, or who had taken their vows under the age of 20, were to be dismissed. The Visitors 'had no scruple about their power to dispense with the solemn obligations of the monastic profession' and dismissed any whom they could persuade to leave. In some instances, only the old and infirm were left. [206]

The visitation lasted until the parliament that opened in February 1536. The results were presented in a black book that 'acknowledged that about a third of the houses, including the bulk of the larger abbeys, were fairly and decently conducted', but 'the rest were charged with drunkenness, with simony, and with the foulest and most revolting crimes'.[207] Whether these were exaggerated or not, parliament subsequently passed the Act of Suppression of the Lesser Monasteries in March 1536.

These 'Lesser Monasteries' were defined as those whose annual income did not exceed £200. By comparison, Reading Abbey's income was just under £2,000 per annum at this date. The need to establish what each religious house was worth, therefore, led to prominent men in each county being commissioned to survey the religious houses in their districts. This, the first wholesale closure of religious houses and confiscation of assets, affected a total of 376 smaller establishments.[208] This wave of closures did not affect any of the Franciscan Houses, in spite of the likelihood of many having an income below £200 per annum. One authority suggests that 'it did not suit the king's purpose to risk the unpopularity of attacking [the friars] when so little was to be gained by so doing'.[209]

This widespread action against the church led to popular

uprisings in 1536, first in Lincolnshire and then in Yorkshire. Before long the whole of the north seemed to be in revolt, known to history as the Pilgrimage of Grace. The king suppressed the risings with over 200 executions, including that of the Pilgrimage's leader Robert Aske. The defeat of the opposition to his suppression of the religious houses caused Henry to aim for much more extensive seizures of monastic and other church property. Consequently, from mid-1538 the friaries were visited and suppressed, with ruthless intent.[210]

The Reading friary was visited by one of the more experienced of Thomas Cromwell's henchmen, Dr John London. London had been one of the four principals in the visitation of 1535 to 1536 mentioned above. He was zealous in the king's service. Gasquet says of him that 'in the work of devastation, London was certainly the most terrible of all the monastic spoilers'.[211]

On the last day of August 1538, Dr London wrote to Cromwell from Oxford. He had successfully closed down the friaries of the Austin, Dominican, Carmelite and Franciscan orders in that city[212], and his sights were set on his next target, Reading's grey friars:

> ...a frynde of myne, the warden of the Grey Fryers in Reding, hathe also desyred me to be an humble sutar for hym and hys brothern, that they may with your lordeschips favour also chaunge ther garmentes with ther papisticall maner of lyvinges. The most partt of them be very agede men, and be nott of strength to go moch abrode for ther lyvinges, wherfor ther desyer ys that yt myght please your lordeschippe to be a mediator unto the kinges grace for them that they myght during ther lyves enjoy ther chambres and orcharde, and they wolde assuredly pray unto almightie Godde long to preserve the kinges grace and your lordeshipp to hys most blessyd pleasure.[213]

The Reading warden, Peter Schefford, would have been in no doubt that it was only a matter of time before his friary's turn came to be dissolved. Already by the end of August well over 30 friaries of the four orders had been suppressed, 13 of them Franciscan. Most of these friaries had been closed by former friar Richard Ingworth, by this time Bishop of Dover. It is a strange coincidence that in the history of the Franciscan friaries in England there were two men named Richard Ingworth. The other was one of the first party of Franciscan friars to land at Dover in 1224. Thus one Richard Ingworth set up several friaries in the 13th century and another Richard Ingworth closed many of them down over 300 years later.

By the time Dr London was in Reading, two more Franciscan friaries – at Cardiff and at Bristol – had been closed by the Bishop of Dover. Reading's friary was therefore the 16th to be closed, dissolved on the same day as the friary at Bridgwater.[214]

Dr London's letter quoted above implies that Peter Schefford, the warden, had asked London to plead with Cromwell that at least the elderly among the brothers at Reading should be allowed to stay on in the friary, even when they were no longer friars, enjoying their chambers and orchard. The *quid pro quo* of the prayers of the ex-friars for the king and for Cromwell would no doubt be balanced against the financial loss to the king if he allowed them to stay in the House. Money talked loudest, and so they were not allowed to stay.

When Dr London visited he had several things to achieve. First, he needed the warden and friars to 'surrender' the friary as if of their own free will. Secondly, he had to ensure that everything of value was sequestrated for the king. Thirdly, he had to desecrate the church to make sure that it would not continue in use.

To achieve his first object, Dr London had a standard form of surrender for the warden and friars to agree and sign. The form of words given below from the Reading House is very similar to those from Aylesbury, Bedford, Coventry and

Stamford (surrendered on the 1, 3, 5 and 8 October 1538 respectively). Dated 13 September 1538, the Act of 'Surrender of the House of Gray-friers, in Reding' states:

Forasmuch as we do now consider, as well by dayly experience, as by example and doctrine of divers well learned persons, which have heretofore professed diverse sorts of pretended religions, that the very true way to perfection and to please God is ministered unto us sincerely and sufficiently by the most wholesome doctrine of Christ, his Evangelists and Apostolis, and after declared by the Holy Fathers in the primitive Church of Christ, and doth not consist in the traditions and inventions of man's witt, in wering of a grey, black, white or any other colored garment, cloke, frock or coate, in garding ourselves upon our outward garments with gurdells full of knotts, or in like peculiar manner of papisticall ceremonies; sequestering ourselves from the uniform, laudable, and conformable manner of liveing of all Christian men, used many yeares from the beginning of Christ's religion. Perceiving, also, that as well the high estates of this realme as the common people doe noote in us, and daylye doth laye unto our charges, the detestable cryme of hypocrisy, dissimulation and superstition, which draweth their benevolence and supportation from us, whereby we have been in tymes past in manner only sustained: We therefore the warden and convent of the house called commonly Grey-Fryers of Reding, considering that we may be the true servants of God, as well in a secular habit as in a fryer's coate, and knowing and well considering the miserable state we stand in, being fully determined in ourselves to leave all such papisticall and strange fashions of lyveing, with the garments appertaining unto the same, with all our mutuall and free assents and consents, doe most humblye in this behalfe submit ourselves and every one of us, our house and place wee dwell in, and all our buildings, ornaments, utensells, juells, tyths, commodities, and all our things, whatsoever they be pertaining unto the same, and by these presents doe surrender the same, and yeilde them up into the hands and disposition of our most noble sovereign Lord the King's Majestie; most humbly beseeching the same, freely and without any charge, in consideration of our extreme poverties, to grant unto every one of us, his letters under writeing and his Grace's seal, to change our said habitts, and to take such manner of living, as honest seculer priests be preferred unto. And wee all shall ffaithfully pray unto Almighty God, long to preserve his most noble Grace. In witness of all the premisses and every part of the same, we have subscribed our names unto these presents, and have put to our common and conventual seal unto the same, the XIII day of ye month of September, and in the XXX yeare of the raigne of our sovereigne lord Henry the VIII.

> Per me Petrum Schefford, Guardianum, STB
> Per me Egidium Coventre, STB
> Per me Henricum Allen
> Per me Petrum Stanch
> Per me Nicolaum Martin
> Per me Robertum Lambert
> Joh'em Newarke
> Will'um Tudbodis
> Joh'em Gruer
> Joh'em Rosell
> Ric'um Leyrston
> Will'um Thompson[215]

It is very notable that this Act of Surrender is signed by the warden and 11 friars, this being just one below the usual capacity of the friary. Elsewhere, the number of friars at a House in 1538 was well below the normal number that the House contained. For example, although Oxford generally had about 80 friars, it had just 18 at its surrender. Gloucester would have had about 40 friars usually, but only 5 when it was closed down. Of the 18 Houses for which there is data at the dissolution and at least one other point, the Reading House is the only one with virtually a complete complement in 1538.[216]

One major reason that the number of friars nationally had fallen by this date was the collapse of local support, leading to a situation where the friars could not subsist. An example of this occurred in Ipswich, where the friars were having to sell off the friary's jewels as 'the warden and brethren lived there in great necessity, for the inhabitants were extending their charity to the poor and impotent instead of to such an idle nest of drones'.[217] Similarly at Shrewsbury, when Ingworth arrived to dissolve the house, he found that 'the Grey Friars had sold everything and were glad to give up'.[218] Clearly this had not been the case in Reading; the friars must have continued to enjoy the support of the local townspeople.

On the next day, Saturday 14 September 1538, Dr London wrote to Thomas Cromwell:

> I have taken a surrender of the friars in Reading, and this day they shall change their coats. "Of friars they be noted here honest men." In the house are three pretty lodgings; the warden keeps one, Mr Ogle, the King's servant, another, and an old lady called my lady Seynt Jone the third. None is out by convent seal, but they say they promised one to Mr Ogle. There is a goodly walk in their back side with trees, ponds and an orchard, in all 20 acres. Household stuff, coarse. What little plate and jewels there is I will send up this week. There is a great trough of lead at their well and another in their kitchen, and the bell turret is covered with lead. Church ornaments slender. The inside of the church and windows, decked with grey friars, I have defaced and yet made some money out of "these things". On Monday I will pay their debts to victuallers and rid the house of them all. Today I will go to Caversham, a mile from Reading, where is a great pilgrimage, and send the image up to your Lordship's place in London. "My Lord here doubteth my being here very sore," yet I have not seen him since I came, nor been at his house except yesterday to hear mass: the last time I was here he said, as they all do, he was at the King's command, but loth be they to come to any free surrender.
> Reading 14 Septembris.
> The bearer, an honest gentleman, has taken pains with me at

the friars. I beg you, thank him.[219]

There is much in this letter of interest. To start near the end, the Lord who 'doubteth my being here very sore' was the abbot of Reading Abbey, Hugh Cook of Faringdon. Dr London was not a welcome visitor to Friday mass.

The lodgings for Mr Ogle and my lady Saint Joan have been mentioned earlier, as examples of a corrody (see page 63). The description of the grounds with a 'goodly walk', trees, ponds and an orchard sound idyllic, although 20 acres was rather an overestimate of what was later to be called 6.

Unfortunately no detailed inventory has survived of the Reading friary's goods. Where such inventories still exist for other friaries, they are very useful in any attempt at reconstructing the interior of the friaries' churches and other buildings. An example from Bridgwater Franciscan friary, surrendered on the same day as Reading, includes:

Choir:- a table of alabaster with 9 images, 2 goodly candlesticks, a pair of organs, an iron grate about a tomb, &c.

Church:- 3 cloths before the altars, a chapel with a frame barred with iron.

Sextry: 21 copes detailed, of velvet, silk &c... a suit of white damask with flowers of gold, a suit of blue silk with stars of gold...[220]

Since Dr London wrote that Reading's 'Household stuff' was 'coarse', perhaps Reading had little or nothing to compare with that at Bridgwater's House. The latter certainly had much more 'plate and jewels' than the Reading House. Bridgwater had 358oz (just over 10kg), while:

The Graye Fryers in Redynge, in gilte plate xiiij oz, in parcel-gilt plate xxxij oz, and in white xl oz, by Indenture of the vth of

October, under thande of the saied Thomas Thacker.[221]

The total weight of this 14oz of gilt plate, 32oz of parcel, or partial, gilt plate and 40oz of white gilt plate is 86oz (just under 2.5kg). It would have been nice to have had a description of the chalices, cups, flagons, plates and so on that this haul consisted of, but we are left to imagine what it might have been.

Dr London's comment 'Church ornaments, slender' also suggests that there was little of value inside the church. Often, elsewhere, the alabaster altars, the statuary and the metal railings around tombs all merit a mention. Perhaps there was little in good condition here.

The stained glass windows ('decked with grey friars') and the lead in the well, the kitchen and the bell tower roof, were all promising items for Dr London to convert to money for his masters, although he was soon to be disappointed in some of it.

The following day, Sunday 15 September 1538, Dr London wrote again to Cromwell:

In my most humble maner I have me comendyd unto yr gudde lordeschippe w^t my assured prayer and service I have sent up to y^r lordeschippe the surrender of the Gray-fryers of Reding w^t ther plait such as yt ys. I have inwardly defacyd the churche and dort^r. The resydew of the house I have left hole til I know yor farther pleasur, and clerly dispacchyd all the friers out of doores in their secular apparell. And have given to every oon of them money in ther purcys, and have clerly payd ther detts. Thys ys a towne of moche pour people, and they fell to steling so fast in every corner of the howse, that I have be fayne to tarry a hole weke here to sett every thing in dew ordre. And have and schall receive to the king's grace's use, I trust Xli. the mansion holy reservyd.[222]

Dr London intended to cast the friars out on Monday 16 September according to his letter of 14 September. I wonder if the friars were allowed to use the defaced quire one last time on Sunday 15 September for their services. There would be no service of divine worship in the building for another 325 years – the next being the nave's rededication as Grey Friars Church on 2 December 1863.[223]

Dr London had significant trouble with theft from the friary by the Reading townspeople. He recurs to the problem in his next letter, which mostly dealt with the removal of 'the image of our ladye at Caversham' and the pulling down of the shrine there. London wrote to Cromwell on Tuesday 17 September 1538:

> I ... have made fast the doores of the chapel [of our Lady at Caversham] wiche ys thorowly well covered with ledde... And, if it be nott so orderyd, the chapell standith so wildely that the ledde will be stolyn by nyght, as I wasse servyd at the Fryers; ffor as soon as I hadde taken the Fryers surrendre, the multytude of the poverty of the town resortyd thedyr, and all thinge myght be hadde they stole away, insomyche that they hadde convayd the very clapers of the bellys. And saving that Mr Fachell, wiche made me great chere at hys howse, and the mayer dydde assist me, they wolde have made no litill spoyle.[224]

'Mr Fachell' was Thomas Vachel, one of the town's two members of parliament, who lived at Coley Park and was Deputy Steward of Reading under Thomas Cromwell. Cromwell had been appointed High Steward of the town by Abbot Hugh earlier in 1538.

The mayor who assisted Dr London was Richard Turner. A mercer by trade, Turner had first been chosen as mayor in September 1523 when proposed by the town's burgesses, together with Richard Barnes and Richard a' Man, to abbot Hugh Cook of Faringdon. The abbot exercised his right to choose the mayor from those candidates offered, and so Richard Turner was installed in office.[225] Turner also served as mayor in 1527, 1531, and in 1535 for the last quarter of the year when mayor Thomas Everard died in office.[226] Turner had been elected for the fifth time in September 1537, and was nearing the end of his tenure when he helped Dr London to stop the poor of the town making off with too many valuables from the friary.

Dr London expressed his gratitude to Turner in his letter to Cromwell quoted above. The mayor lost no time in trying to gain an advantage for the town from being in London's good books. He requested that they be allowed to have the nave of the friary church for a town hall.

London continued in his letter to Cromwell:

I besek your gudde lordeschippe to admytt me a power sutar [poor suitor] for thees honest men of Redinge. They have a fayer towne and many gudde occupiers in ytt, butt they lacke that howse necessary, of the wiche, for the mynystracion of justice, they have most nede of. Ther towne hall ys a very small howse, and stondith upon the ryver, wher ys the commyn wassching place of the most partt of the towne, and in the cession dayes and other cowrt dayes ther ys such betyng with batildores as oon man can nott here another nor the quest here the chardg gevyng.

The body of the Church of the Grey Fryers, wiche ys solyd with lath and lyme, wold be a very commodiose rowme for them. And now I have rydde all the fasschen of that Church in parcleses [screens], ymages, and awlters, it wolde make a gudly towne hall. The mayer of that towne, Mr. Richard Turner, is a very honest gentill person, with many other honest men, hathe expressyd unto me ther gref in thys behalf, and have desyred me to be an humble sutar unto your lordeschippe for the same, if it shulde be solde. The wallys besyd the coyne stonys be butt chalk

and flynt, and the coveryng butt tile. And if it please the kinges
grace to bestow that howse upon any of hys servantes, he may
spare the body of the churche, wiche stondith next the strete,
very well, and yt have rowme sufficient for a great man.

Your most bounden oratour and servant,
John London.[227]

The town's Guildhall, here described as a very small house
that stands upon the river, had been built in 1420 on an island
that was accessed by footbridge at the end of George Lane,
roughly where Yield Hall Place is now. Its proximity to the
washer women with their noisy 'batildores', which were
wooden implements for beating clothes, meant that it had
proved to be less than ideal for the transaction of guild
business.

His work completed, Dr London left Reading soon after,
heading for the friary at Aylesbury. However, he did return to
Reading less than five years later under quite different
conditions. He fell out of favour at court after Cromwell's
death and was convicted of perjury, then stripped of all his
titles and positions. He was then made to ride through
Reading facing the horse's tail and put in the pillory with a
notice declaring his crime on his forehead. After having to do
the same in Newbury and Windsor, he was imprisoned in The
Fleet, where he died in 1543.[228]

Unfortunately nothing is known about what happened to
most of the friars after they were cast out from the friary. In
the parish records of St Mary's Church, there is a John Russell
who was buried on 24 May 1559, who may have been the
'Joh'em Rosell' named on the surrender document in 1538.

The friars, having taken a vow of poverty, rarely received
more than a little cash 'in their purses' when they took
'secular apparel', unlike monks, who were usually awarded a
pension by the crown. If the friar was a priest then there was

the possibility of a benefice, as certainly happened for some. However,

> what proportion these successful cases bore to the unsuccessful cannot be even approximately ascertained; it would naturally be higher among friars who had received a university education than among the common herd. Yet it is unlikely that a majority even of the former were presented to livings. The number of disbanded monks and friars seeking employment as priests must have been very large, and at the same time the demand for priests was growing less and less. Some of the friars probably drifted into secular employment; others perhaps joined the ranks of the 'study beggars' of whom so much is heard in the sixteenth century. It can hardly be doubted but that the lot of many was one of hardship and suffering.[229]

At their greatest number, there had been about 1,700 Franciscan friars in England. This had fallen to about 600 by the time of the dissolution. As the ecclesiastical historian John Moorman put it: 'the whole Franciscan community ... quietly disappeared from the English scene, leaving little behind it except a few fragmentary remains ... to show what, at one time, had been a noble and vigorous element in the spiritual life of the country'.[230]

A little more is known about Peter Schefford, the warden, and Giles Coventry, sub-warden, of the Reading House. They are both named in a document dated 20 November 1539 that contains a list of prisoners in the Tower of London.

> The prisoners' names that be in the Tower on the 20th day of November in the 31st year of the reign of our Sovereign lord king Henry VIII... Roger London, monk of Reading, Peter Lorance, which was warden of the Grey Friars in Reading, Giles Coventre, which was a friar of the same house ...[231]

It is clear from this that Peter Schefford, warden of Grey Friars, Reading, at the dissolution had an alias of Peter Lorence, or Lawrence.

Five days earlier, Hugh Cook of Faringdon, Abbot of Reading Abbey, John Eynon and John Rugg had suffered the death of traitors by the Abbey's Gateway. Before that they would also have been prisoners in the Tower. The abbot:

> standing in the space before the gateway of his abbey, spoke to the people who in great numbers had gathered to witness the strange spectacle of the execution of a lord abbot of the great and powerful monastery of Reading. He told them the cause for which he and his companions were to die, not fearing openly to profess that which Henry's laws made it treason to hold – fidelity to the see of Rome...[232]

In a partially damaged 33 page document, summarised in the *Letters and Papers, Foreign and Domestic, Henry VIII*, under the heading of Treason, the writer of the 'discourse' refers to the abbot of Reading's 'followers', imprisoned in the Tower of London, by name, including 'Bachelar Gyles' and 'the warden of the friars'.[233] This allows us to make the identification of Giles Coventry with Bachelor Giles. We know already from his signature on the suppression document that Giles was an STB, and so a Bachelor of Sacred Theology, and therefore the name would be appropriate.[234] Some years later, in a letter to the Bishop of Norwich about a prisoner captured and examined to see if he was a papist, Dr Gardiner, a former Chancellor of England, wrote:

> He [Sir Peter Kilburne, the prisoner] confesseth that he sent him [Mr Cotton, another suspect] a book made by one Bachelor

Giles, sometime a frier in Norwich, against the King's Supremacy and in defence of the Pope's Jurisdiction... [235]

Giles Coventry had been warden of Walsingham before coming to Reading, and so may well also have been resident at nearby Norwich. Perhaps he had even left Norfolk to escape notice of the authorities following the writing of this, as Henry would view it, treasonous book.

Although it is not certain, it is very likely that Giles Coventry was released from the Tower, as in June 1544 a person of that name was appointed sub-dean of the Guild College in Stratford–upon–Avon, being in that role until the end of the following year.[236]

However, it is not known what happened to the last warden of Grey Friars, Reading, Peter Schefford, alias Lawrence. He may well have followed the abbot of Reading Abbey to the hangman's gibbet.

View of the nave

Greyfriars Church, Reading,

following reordering in 2000

Chapter 9

Disposal and Afterwards

The king aimed to make money from the assets seized from the religious houses. On 5 February 1540, Henry granted the buildings and site of the friary to Robert Stanshawe for an initial payment of £30 and an annual rent of 6s 8d, this being a twentieth of a 'knight's fee'.[237] The grant did not include the nave of the friary church, and so Stanshawe received everything else within the perimeter wall, namely:

> the whole house and site of the Friers minors, commonly called the Grey-friers in Redyng, in the county of Berks, the whole burial-place, houses, buildings, orchards, gardens, lands, tenements, trees, woods, lakes, vineyards, with all and singular the appurtenances thereunto belonging, and also the site, extent and precinct, walls and ditches, of the aforesaid house of the friers minors late so called, being round about, and adjoining to the same, and the site and precinct of the house, including and containing in the whole, by estimation, six acres. [238]

Dr London had removed everything of value and had defaced and destroyed much, especially of the church buildings. The property was still, however, very valuable, although it seems unlikely that there were vineyards as described above, and for 'lakes' read ponds.

Robert Stanshawe was a groom of the king's chamber and therefore a member of the royal household, personally known to the king. Robert was a local man who held various plots of land in the area, including a farm in Streatley, 16 acres in King's Mead, and farmland in Battle.[239] His acquisition of the friary included the quire of the church, within which his father, John Stanshawe, had been buried (see page 78).

Robert took up residence in the old friary, as can be seen from his will, dated 28 August 1549, where his house is 'called the Fryars in Redyng'. The will is accompanied by an inventory of the house, dated 27 September 1549, listing a hall, parlour, great parlour, two bedrooms (one called the great chamber), a maid servant's bedroom, a buttery and a kitchen.[240] Robert died in 1551.

Some later owners of the old friary land and buildings are given in Coates: William Webb and Wolfstan Dixey in 1576/7 and John Carleton in 1614/15.[241] While in the latter's ownership, Queen Anne of Denmark, wife of James I, stayed for the night at the 'Fryers', on her way from London to Bath:

At this daye the said Capitall Burgesses had in remembrance the cominge of the Queene to the Towne, provision beinge made for her staye at the Fryers for one daye and night as she was goeing to Bath; and it was considered what was fit to be done by the Company at her Majesties cominge; and it was then concluded that the Company should then attend and shewe themselves in dutie, but not geve any present unlesse they shalbe advised soe to doe by the Lord Knolles, beinge Highe Steward.[242]

About 1640 part of the land had passed into the ownership of Tanfield Vachel. When he died in 1658 he bequeathed his land 'near Reading called Potmon Brooke' to his sister Elizabeth, wife of Alexander Thistlethwayte.[243] In turn the land passed to Dorothy Vachel, widow of another Tanfield Vachel, and their son Thomas.

Both Robert Stanshawe and the Vachels are commemorated in roads built in the late 1850s on the old friary land between Caversham Road and Greyfriars Road.

In the early 18th century the various parts of the old friary land were bought up by John Dalby, a prominent local man who was the Recorder of Reading from 1686 to 1687 and 1688 to 1720, and Member of Parliament for Reading from 1698 to 1700 and 1710 to 1713. Together with Anthony Blagrave he had owned the abbey ruins and land, but had sold his share to Henry Vansittart.

Dalby bought the house called the Fryers and its surroundings from his brother Edward. This was probably the land in the south west corner where the main friary buildings were built. He also bought Fryers Garden from Elizabeth Downing, widow, and her son William. This consisted of the east part of the land, stretching down to the Portman Brook. The remaining section, known as Fryers Ground, was a 6 acre plot including 'the Orchard' and (surprisingly) a bowling alley. Fryers Ground stretched from the Caversham Road (to the north of the Fryers) to the 'Fosterns', or Vasterns on the north. Dalby bought this land from Dorothy Vachel, Thomas Vachel, Richard Neville and Thomas Holby.[244]

John Dalby died in October 1720, and in August 1722 his heirs sold the whole area to Joseph Heycock, an apothecary.

Subsequently, the area became known as 'Heycock's Fryars', and the land stayed in the Heycock family until the beginning of the 19th century. In 1806 Lancelot Austwick, a wine merchant, alderman and past and future mayor of Reading (1803–4 and 1812–13), purchased the land, buying up several tenancies at the same time to create an estate of about 14 acres. Austwick cleared the land of various buildings and created gardens and walks, with a newly built house fronting Friar Street. This house, which became the Greyfriars Church vicarage, is generally thought to have been designed by Sir John Soane, but it was not.[245]

Lancelot Austwick died in 1829 and the 'Grey Friars Estate' as it began to be grandly called was again split several ways with most of the area being owned by John Weedon and by Francis Morgan Slocombe. A large part of it was sold off to the Corporation in order to create Tudor Road, Stanshawe Road and Vachel Road by about 1860. Sackville Street was built about 1881.

Having followed the history of the buildings and land sold to Robert Stanshawe, we come to the part held back by Henry VIII. Perhaps surprisingly, the king agreed to let the Corporation have the nave of the church to use as a Guildhall.

On 24 April 1542, Henry granted Reading a new Charter, which included the following:

> Know ye that we of our special grace have granted and by these presents for us our heirs and successors grant to the said Mayor and Burgesses of Reading aforesaid and their successors for ever the body and side aisles of the said Church and one competent and sufficient road to the same.[246]

The initial charge was to be the hundredth part of one knight's fee (16d) and an annual peppercorn rent of one halfpenny, payable on the feast of St. Michael the Archangel (29 September). The Mayor and Burgesses were then 'at their own expense, [to] make and construct or cause to be made and constructed from the same a sufficient house there commonly called Le Gyldhawle for the said town'.

The church building was used as a Guildhall for 35 years or so until about 1578, at which time the Corporation moved to the old Abbey Hospitium, next to St Laurence's Church. In 1560, the Charter of Queen Elizabeth presented the former friary nave to the Corporation as their own possession, with the right to use it as they wished. It was first used as a kind of workhouse, known as the Hospital for the 'deserving poor', and subsequently part of it was converted to be a House of Correction, a type of prison, for the 'undeserving poor'.

After housing a garrison of troops in the Civil War the former church building became just a prison, known as a Bridewell by the 18th century. Almost 350 years after the dissolution it was finally converted back to a church and rededicated on 2 December 1863 as Grey Friars, now Greyfriars, Church.[247] It is now a thriving church which aims to serve the local community in Reading, in the spirit of those same grey friars of the 13th to 16th centuries.

Greyfriars Church, Reading
celebrating 700 years in 2011

Wardens and Friars of the Reading House

Wardens (with known dates)

1320	Warner
1327	William de Assewell
1492	William
1516	John Thacham
1531–1538	Peter Schefford STB (also known as Peter Lorence or Laurence)

Friars (with known dates)

1328	John de Bokingham
1328	John de Graue
1328	Richard de Waneting
1328	William de Abindon
1328	William de Okam
1333	Helias de Aylesbirye
1350s–1362	John Lathbury DD
1413	William Boteler DD
Late 1440s	Thomas Radnor DD
1489	William Wursley (possibly the same as William, the Warden in 1492, above)

1516	Henry Aleyn
1538	Giles Coventry STB
1538	Henry Allen (possibly the same as Henry Aleyn above)
1538	John Gruer
1538	John Newarke
1538	John Rosell
1538	Nicholas Martin
1538	Peter Stanch
1538	Richard Leyrston
1538	Robert Lambert
1538	William Thompson
1538	William Tudbodis

Bibliography

J. H. E. Bennett, *The Grey Friars of Chester* in *The Chester Archaeological Society's Journal Volume XXIV, Part I* (Chester 1921)

John Billings, *On the History and Remains of the Franciscan Friery, Reading* in *The Archaeological Journal*, Volume III (London 1846) pages 141–148

William Moir Bryce, *The Scottish Grey Friars*, Volume 1 History (Sands & Co., Edinburgh & London 1909)

Calendar of the Charter Rolls preserved in the Public Record Office Several volumes (HMSO, London 1903 and later)

Calendar of the Close Rolls preserved in the Public Record Office Several volumes (HMSO, London 1905 and later)

Calendar of Fine Rolls preserved in the Public Record Office Several Volumes (HMSO, London 1911 and later)

Calendar of the Liberate Rolls preserved in the Public Record Office Several volumes (HMSO, London 1916 and later)

David Carpenter, *Magna Carta* (Penguin, London 2015)

Rev. Charles Coates, *The History and Antiquities of Reading* (J. Nichols & Son, London 1802)

Charles Cotton, *The Grey Friars of Canterbury 1224 to 1538* (Longmans, Green & Co., Manchester 1926)

John Doran, *The History and Antiquities of the Town and Borough of Reading in Berkshire* (Samuel Reader, Reading 1835)

The Chronicle of Thomas Eccleston or *De Adventu Fratrum Minorum in Angliam,* translated by Father Cuthbert O.S.F.C. (Sands & Co., Edinburgh & London, 1909)

Francis Aidan Gasquet, *Henry VIII and the English Monasteries* Volume I (John Hodges, London 1888) and Volume II (John Hodges, London 1889)

Rev. J. M. Guilding (Ed.), *Reading Records: Diary of the Corporation* in Volume 1 (1431–1602) (James Parker & Co., London 1892) and Volume 2 (1603-1629) (James Parker & Co., London 1895)

Rev. Charles Hole, *The Life of the Reverend and Venerable William Whitmarsh Phelps* Volume 2 (Hatchards, London 1873)

A L Humphreys, *Caversham Bridge 1231–1926* (E. Poynder & Son, Reading 1926)

Jamieson Boyd Hurry, *Reading Abbey* (Elliot Stock, London 1901)

Jamieson Boyd Hurry, *The Octocentenary of Reading Abbey* (Elliot Stock, London 1921)

Edward Hutton, *The Franciscans in England 1224–1538* (Constable & Co., London 1926)

Brian R Kemp (Ed.), *Reading Abbey Cartularies* Volume 2 (Royal Historical Society, London 1987)

Brian R Kemp, *Reading Abbey Records: A New Miscellany* (Berkshire Record Society Volume 25, 2018)

Rev Charles Kerry, *A History of the Municipal Church of St Lawrence, Reading* (Reading 1883)

C. L. Kingsford (Ed.), *Collectanea Franciscana II* (Manchester 1922)

Letters and Papers, Foreign and Domestic, of the Reign of Henry VIII Several Volumes (HMSO, London 1862 and later)

A. G. Little, *The Grey Friars in Oxford* (Clarendon Press, Oxford 1892)

A. G. Little, *Records of the Franciscan Province of England* in *Collectanea Franciscana I* (Aberdeen 1914)

A. G. Little, *Studies in English Franciscan History* (Longmans, Green & Co., Manchester 1917)

A. G. Little (Ed.), *Franciscan History and Legend in English Mediaeval Art* (Manchester University Press, 1937)

Henry Richards Luard (Ed.), *Annales Monastici* Volume 3 (Longman's, Green, Reader and Dyer, London 1866)

John Man, *The History and Antiquities, Ancient and Modern, of the Borough of Reading, in the County of Berks* (Snare & Man, Reading 1816)

A. R. Martin, *Franciscan Architecture in England* (The University Press, Manchester 1937)

John R H Moorman, *The Franciscans in England 1224-1538* (Mowbrays, Oxford 1974)

Anthony Parkinson, *Collectanea Anglo-Minoritica: Or A Collection of the Antiquities of the English Franciscans, or Friers Minors, Commonly called Gray Friers* (Thomas Smith, London 1726) In two parts.

Nikolaus Pevsner, Geoffrey Tyack & Simon Bradley, *The Buildings of England: Berkshire* (Yale University Press, New Haven and London 2010)

Kenneth W Rowlands, *The Friars: A History of the British Medieval Friars* (The Book Guild, Lewes 1999)

Malcolm Summers, *History of Greyfriars Church, Reading* (Downs Way Publishing, Reading 2013)

Malcolm Summers, *Signs of the Times: Reading's Memorials* (Two Rivers Press, Reading 2019)

G. E. Weare, *A Collectanea Relating to the Bristol Friars Minors (Gray Friars) and their Convent* (W. Bennett, Bristol 1893)

D. P. Wright (Ed.), *The Register of Thomas Langton, Bishop of Salisbury 1485-93 Part CXLVII Volume LXXIV* (Printed for the Canterbury & York Society 1985)

Thomas Wright, *Three Chapters of Letters relating to the Suppression of the Monasteries* (John Bowyer Nichols & Son, London 1843)

Endnotes & Sources

[1] Moorman p38

[2] Ibid. p62

[3] Liberate Rolls 11 Henry III m.13 (25 December 1226). This is in Volume 1 p11; other occasions before 1233 are given in pp13, 48, 75f, 114, 124, 157, 170, 174–177

[4] Hurry 1901 pp33 and 149

[5] Parkinson p6f gives a good overview of the possible dates

[6] Bryce p5

[7] Hutton p72; Moorman p21; Martin p6–9

[8] Bennett p11–15. This contains the full text both in Latin and translated to English of Grosseteste's letter

[9] Yorkshire Archaeological Society Journal 1935 part 3, article *Franciscans and Dominicans in Yorkshire – Part One The Grey Friars*, chapter 6 The Grey Friars at Scarborough p310–319

[10] Eccleston p25, Little 1892 p180, Parkinson p38

[11] Martin p125

[12] Luard p134, *Annales Prioratus De Dunstaplia* entry for 1233

[13] Ibid. With thanks to Eleanor Summers for the translation from Latin

[14] Charter Rolls 17 Henry III m.2d (14 July 1233); Kemp 1987 pp207f. British Library Cotton Vespasian E xxv fol.217a. Coates p299 and (in Latin) Appendix II. Eccleston p155

[15] Close Rolls 15 Henry III (2 May 1231). Humphreys p7f, and see the facsimile of the Close Roll facing p8

[16] Carpenter p51

[17] *Geometrei. Von künstlichem Feldmessen und absehen* by Jacob Koebel, quoted in Wikipedia article on Foot (Unit) [Accessed January 2019]

[18] Little 1937 p49f, and Ch IV Pl 24; Hutton p169; Rowlands p158

[19] Little 1917 p109 n2

[20] Eccleston p103

[21] Martin p10; Rowlands p97; Cotton p14. Lincoln seems to have been an exception to this as its structure of 'ragstone rubble with freestone dressings' dates from the mid-1200s – see Martin p94

[22] Martin p242

[23] Cotton p29 and fn. 1, quoting *Speculum Perfectionis* (Ed. P. Sabatier, 1898)

[24] Little 1892 p22

[25] Close Rolls 18 Henry III m.25 (2 May 1234)

[26] Ibid. m.17 (28 June 1234)

[27] Martin p14

[28] Liberate Rolls 21 Henry III m.3 (29 August 1237)

[29] Close Rolls 22 Henry III m.15 (29 April 1238). Liberate Rolls 22 Henry III m.7 (29 April 1238)

[30] Liberate Rolls 23 Henry III m.8 (1 August 1239)

[31] Ibid. m.6 (27 August 1239)

[32] Ibid. 24 Henry III m.18 (10 February 1240)

[33] Eccleston p102; Hutton p62. Also see Rev J. Silvester Davies, *A History of Southampton*, Southampton 1883 p442

[34] Eccleston p103; Little 1917 p62

[35] Liberate Rolls 30 Henry III m.17 (29 February 1246 (sic))

[36] Ibid. 23 Henry III m.3 (12 October 1239). Note that the published *Calendar of Liberate Rolls* Henry III Volume 1 AD 1226-1240 (London HMSO 1916) p420 has an error, saying for twelve friars minors. However, the original has the Roman numeral xiij and so 13. See Martin p107 fn.11

[37] Little 1917 p69

[38] Eccleston p13

[39] Hutton p95; Rowlands p368

[40] Little 1917 p58

[41] Ibid. p57

[42] See Cotton p17. When buildings began to be of stone, perimeter walls were built in place of the ditch and palisade

[43] Liberate Rolls 23 Henry III m.6 (27 August 1239)

[44] Ibid. 24 Henry III m.2 (23 October? 1240)

[45] Ibid. 26 Henry III m.15 (6 December 1241)

[46] My thanks to Craig Hampton, Technical Specialist with the Environment Agency, for information about the location of the Portman Brook's modern day successor, the Vastern Ditch, and the impact on the position of the first friary due to the flood zones of the Thames

[47] Little 1917 p57

[48] Liberate Rolls 28 Henry III m.11 (9 May 1244)

[49] Ibid. 32 Henry III m.7 (16 May 1248)

[50] Ibid. 30 Henry III m.17 (14 February 1246)

[51] Ibid. 28 Henry III m.10 (9 May 1244)

[52] Ibid. m.7 (5 July 1244)

[53] Close Rolls 31 Henry III m.6 (25 June 1247)

[54] Ibid. 41 Henry III m.5 (30 June 1257)

[55] Ibid. 42 Henry III m.4 (12 August 1258)

[56] Ibid. 43 Henry III m.12 (6 March 1259)

[57] Ibid. 44 Henry III m.3 (23 September 1260)

[58] Ibid. 8 Edward I m.5 (27 June 1280)

[59] Kemp 2018 p39

[60] Parkinson p84; Coates p251; Hurry 1901 p36

[61] *Registrum Epistolarum Fratris Johannis Peckham, archiepiscopi Cantuariensis* f.105. This is given in full (in Latin) in Coates, Appendix III. Also see Coates p300f

[62] Coates p301. The original is from *Registrum Epistolarum Fratris Johannis Peckham, archiepiscopi Cantuariensis* f.118b. It is also given in full (in Latin) in Coates, Appendix III

[63] Close Rolls 14 Edward I m.2d (25 May 1285). The document is also given (in Latin) in Coates Appendix IV from British Museum Cotton Manuscript Vespasian E.25 fol.27. See also Kemp 1987 p209f and Coates p299f

[64] Kemp 1987 p140f, 212; Fine Rolls 15 Edward I m.4 (8 September 1287)

[65] Coates p300. The will is in the British Library, Cotton Vespasian E v fol. 55

[66] Mary Russell Mitford, *Belford Regis or Sketches of a Country Town* (London 1835) Volume 1 p172 and Volume 2 p103 and p93

[67] *The Journal of the Berkshire Archaeological Association* (London 1860) p239f. Also see *The Builder* Volume XVII No. 868 of 24 September 1859, in an article entitled *Archaeologists in Berkshire – Relics in Reading*

[68] Summers 2013 p75

[69] Hole p217

[70] Close Rolls 31 Edward I m.19 (11 January 1303). Coates p300 (and others who have followed him) quoted this as 33 Edward I, on

11 January 1306. Coates also incorrectly calls the earl of Lincoln Robert de Lacy

[71] Coates p300

[72] See Kemp 1987 p166; Coates p300. The will is in the British Library Cotton Vespasian E xxv fol.189

[73] British Library reference Add MS 36433 No. 496, Buckler Architectural Drawings Volume LXXIX Miscellaneous Volume IV

[74] Billings p146

[75] With thanks to John Missenden

[76] Rowlands p37

[77] From Martin facing p116

[78] Martin p76 shows a plan of the Coventry House which has both north and south transepts, called 'valences'. Martin explains 'The word 'valence' is rarely met with as an architectural term and its exact significance is doubtful, but it appears in friars' churches to have normally denoted the space in front of the nave altars, which would have been enclosed by a screen'. To all intents and purposes, these were transepts! For the altar in the Reading House's north-east see page 78

[79] Little 1937 p23

[80] *Letters and Papers, Foreign and Domestic, of the reign of Henry VIII* 30 Henry VIII (14 September 1538) Dr. John London to Cromwell

[81] Pevsner p446

[82] Man p291

[83] Billings p145–146

[84] Ibid. p146

[85] Ibid. p145

[86] Man p291

[87] Martin p19

[88] For Greyfriars' measurements see Man p291. For Reading Abbey's size see Hurry 1901 p4, using earlier measurements by F. W. Albury

[89] Doran p109; also see Coates p308 and Man p291

[90] Professor E. W. Tristram in in the chapter *Franciscan Influence in English Mediaeval Wall Painting* in Little 1937, p5-10

[91] *Reading Mercury* 21 June 1862 p5 column 4

[92] *Berkshire Chronicle* 5 December 1863 p5 column 1

[93] These are the only types that were found. A report of the tiles in Martin p116 includes a lion in the list of tiles found, but this is incorrect. This error then found its way into Little 1937 p119

[94] Billings p146

[95] Man p291

[96] Billings p145

[97] Summers 2013 p84 and pp123–124

[98] *Berkshire Chronicle* 5 December 1863 p5 column 1. This article summarises the restoration work over the previous 20 months, in a report of the consecration of the Church on 2 December 1863

[99] The Berkshire Archaeological Journal Volume 61 (1963-4) p106

[100] Report of the finding of the doorway arch in 2000 given orally to the author by an eyewitness, a former churchwarden. For a Franciscan friary with a crypt – see details about Great Yarmouth in Martin p152

[101] Rowlands p163

[102] Little 1937 p25 'Many seculars desired to be buried in a friar's habit as a kind of passport to heaven'. Also see Rowlands p162-3 and Hutton p169

[103] Martin p25

[104] See the detail from the will of John Stanshawe given on page 78

[105] Rowlands p171

[106] Little 1917 p73

[107] Parkinson, Part 2 p26, Part 1 p175. This may of course have simply meant it was Franciscan, but as his book is on the subject of Franciscan foundations he mostly uses just 'convent' to refer to them, with the fact that they are Franciscan being understood

[108] Coates p300

[109] Parkinson Part 2 is a good source for these, with additions from Hutton, Martin and Victoria County Histories. Note that there is an uncertainty about Southampton's dedication: Parkinson Part 2 p12 says to St Mary, but the more recent scholarship of Hutton p63 states St Francis. Similarly Chichester may have been dedicated to St Peter (see Parkinson Part 2 p14) but Martin p55 calls this 'doubtful' as the title is given as St Francis in several other places

[110] Doran p108

[111] Kemp 2018 p53–99

[112] The decision was the Papal Bull *Nimis iniqua* dated 28 August 1231, referred to in Hutton p33 and its fn 1

[113] Article by A. G. Little entitled *The Administrative Divisions of the Mendicant Orders in England* in *The English Historical Review* Volume 34 (1919) p205

[114] As mentioned in the text the list of Custodies and Houses changed over time, but this represents the list as most often given. See for example Hutton pp61 to 94, Martin p275 and Parkinson part 2 p1. There were some very short lived Franciscan friaries that are not mentioned in the custody list: Romney (about 1241–87), Maidstone (about 1331–45), Plymouth (from 1383). Although Durham is in the list, it too only lasted a few years (from 1239). There were three Scottish Franciscan friaries that were never included in the English Province: Lanark, Inverkeithing and Kirkcudbright, as these were founded after the Scottish Houses of the English Province were transferred to a Scottish 'vicariate' in 1329. Berwick, like the town it was part of, was sometimes in England and sometimes in Scotland!

[115] Little 1917 p66, Rowlands p73

[116] The main reference is Little 1914 pp145–147. The locations (and frequencies) are: London (11), Oxford (8), Cambridge (6), Stamford (5), Coventry (4), Lincoln (4), Nottingham (3), Gloucester (2), Leicester (2), Salisbury (2), then once each at Bedford, Bridgwater, Bristol, Bury St Edmund, Canterbury, Southampton, Worcester and York

[117] Martin p243, and see footnotes 12 and 13 on that page

[118] Little 1917 p102

[119] Coates p304, Martin p127

[120] See Bryce

[121] List Entry Number 1321952. See https://historicengland.org.uk/ [Accessed July 2019]

[122] Little 1892 p91

[123] Dugdale's *Warwickshire*, printed in 1656, quoted in Parkinson Part 1 p37

[124] Martin p5

[125] Little 1917 p133. Also see Rowlands p179

[126] Quoted in Little 1917 p134 from *Robert Grosseteste Epistolae*

[127] Little 1937 Chapter IV Plate 15

[128] Moorman p38

[129] Little 1917 p127

[130] Moorman p66

[131] Little 1917 p116, referring to the lists of friars given in Little 1914 pages 141-153

[132] Little 1917 p107

[133] Cotton p45. This Bull was revoked by Pope Benedict XI in 1304, but reinstated by Clement V in 1312

[134] Little 1882 p110

[135] *Letters and Papers, Foreign and Domestic, of the reign of Henry VIII* 30 Henry VIII (14 September 1538)

[136] Little 1892 pages 43 to 47

[137] Sarum Episcopal Register: Mortival ii fol. 186

[138] Quoted in Little 1892 p44 fn 1

[139] Little 1914 in *British Society of Franciscan Studies* Volume V, Collectanea Franciscana I Ed. AG Little MR James HM Bannister (Aberdeen 1914) pp141–151

[140] This is not the famous William of Ockham, who was a contemporary and a Franciscan friar, who lived until 1347, having been a professor of philosophy at Avignon in 1327-8

[141] Hutton p177

[142] Ibid. pp172–180

[143] Parkinson Part 1 p187–8

[144] Little 1892 p235 fn 4 and p236. Parkinson Volume 1 p187 gives his death date as 1406.

[145] Parkinson Part 1 p175

[146] Quoted in Parkinson Part 2 p26

[147] Berkshire Record Office D/ED/F139. With thanks to Joe Chick for this reference and the translation from Latin

[148] Parkinson pp191–193. Also see Little 1892 p254–5

[149] Little 1892 p255 fn 5, quoting *Illustrium Majoris Britanniae Scriptorum* by John Bale, 1559

[150] The National Archives Prerogative Court of Canterbury Wills PROB 11/3/47. With thanks to Joe Chick for this reference and the translation from Latin

[151] Parkinson Part 1 p198; Little 1892 p258 and 260. For a list of Ministers-Provincial of England see English Historical Review October 1891, where Radnor is 37th in the list. Parkinson Part 1 p xii has Br Thomas Raidnor D.D. at 48th in the list

[152] Berkshire Record Office R/AT1/202

[153] The National Archives Prerogative Court of Canterbury Wills PROB 11/6/349

[154] *The Quarterly Journal of the Berkshire Archaeological and Architectural Society* Volume ii, No. 7, October 1892, p150; The National Archives Prerogative Court of Canterbury Wills PROB 11/6/430

[155] Summers 2019 p4–6

[156] D. P. Wright entry 569

[157] The National Archives Prerogative Court of Canterbury Wills PROB 11/9/40

[158] Guilding v1 pages 35, 47, 50–54. Also Coates Appendix XIII and XIV

[159] Berkshire Record Office D/EBz T1/6

[160] From Arthur L. Humphreys, *Bucklebury: A Berkshire Parish: the Home of Bolingbroke 1701-1715* (Reading 1932) p132

[161] Bennett p19, quoting *Monumenta Franciscana* (Rolls Series) Volume 2 p xxxi

[162] Guilding v1 p82; Coates Appendix XIII

[163] The National Archives Prerogative Court of Canterbury Wills PROB 11/10/70. The full transcription is given in Kerry pp168–173. Kelsall died by early 1494 as his will was proved in either January or February that year

[164] Kerry p17, 84–86, 223. The bell was recast in 1567

[165] The National Archives Prerogative Court of Canterbury Wills PROB 11/11/369. With thanks to Joe Chick for this reference and the translation from Latin

[166] *The Berks, Bucks & Oxon Archaeological Journal* Volume 5, No. 1, April 1899, p50 'The Will of Nicholas Carewe', proved on 10 May 1458

[167] D. P. Wright entry 80: "Institution of Thomas Empster, chaplain to Sulham Church vacant by resignation of William Ringesall; patrons William Twyneo, armiger, and Margaret his wife. Sonning

1st September 1486." Also entry 185: "Institution of M. Thomas Henbury Chaplain to Sulham Church vacant by resignation of Thomas Empstar; patrons William Twyneo, armiger, and Margaret his wife. 31st October 1488."

[168] D. P. Wright entry 538. See also Coates p302 and John Hutchins, *The History and Antiquities of the County of Dorset*, Volume 2 (London 1774) p171. Both Coates and Hutchins call Margaret's husband Thomas

[169] The National Archives Prerogative Court of Canterbury Wills PROB 11/13/171. The will is partially transcribed in *The Berks, Bucks & Oxon Archaeological Journal* Volume 5, No. 1, April 1899, p49–50

[170] Coates p302

[171] Summers 2013 p48

[172] *The Berks Bucks & Oxon Archaeological Journal* Vol 6 No 1 Apr 1900 p25; The National Archives Prerogative Court of Canterbury Wills PROB 11/25/106

[173] The National Archives Prerogative Court of Canterbury Wills: John Love PROB 11/13/544; John Wilcox PROB 11/15/461; and Christian Nicholas PROB 11/16/321. With thanks to Joe Chick for the references

[174] Coates Appendix No. XIII and XIV; Hurry 1901 p60–1

[175] The National Archives Prerogative Court of Canterbury Wills PROB 11/17

[176] The National Archives Prerogative Court of Canterbury Wills PROB 11/18/366. With thanks to Joan Dils for the reference

[177] The National Archives Prerogative Court of Canterbury Wills PROB 11/19. A brief summary of this will can be found in *The Quarterly Journal of the Berks Archaeological and Architectural Society* Volume 3 No. 4 p103

[178] The National Archive PROB 11/21. With thanks to Joe Chick for this reference

[179] Coates Appendix No XIII

[180] Ibid. Appendix No XIV

[181] The National Archives Prerogative Court of Canterbury Wills PROB 11/20/131. With thanks to Joe Chick for this reference

[182] Ibid. 11/20/296. With thanks to Joe Chick for this reference

[183] Ibid. 11/22/545. With thanks to Joe Chick for this reference

[184] Coates Appendix No. XIII and XIV

[185] See Kerry p116–117

[186] The National Archives Prerogative Court of Canterbury Wills PROB 11/25/281. See also Kerry p175–6 and a brief summary of this will can be found in *The Quarterly Journal of the Berks Archaeological and Architectural Society* Volume 3 No. 6 p150–1

[187] The National Archive PROB 11/27/152. Sir Thomas Englefield Jun. died on 28 September 1537.

[188] Coates Appendix No XIV. Watts was mayor in 1512–3, 1517–8 and 1518–9

[189] The National Archives Prerogative Court of Canterbury Wills PROB 11/25/408. See Kerry p177–8

[190] Kingsford p140–141. The National Archives Prerogative Court of Canterbury Wills PROB 11/27/153

[191] John Leland, *Antiquarii De Rebus Britannicis Collectanea* Volume IV (London 1770) p57

[192] Little 1892 p150

[193] Leland *op. cit.* Volume III p60, quoted in Little 1892 p62

[194] Letters and Papers, Foreign and Domestic, 27 Henry VIII, Volume 10 (22 April 1536) 709

[195] Ibid. 28 Henry VIII, Volume 12 Part 1 (15 April 1537) 947

[196] Ibid. 29 Henry VIII, Volume 12 Part 1 (30 April 1537) 1068

[197] British Library reference Add MS 14282 *Berkshire Illustration: Drawings of Ancient Seals* f.8 by B. Howlett 1823. Gabriel on the left, Our Lady on the right, between them a lily in a pot. This design is also used on the warden's seal in Berwick and the custodian's seal in Oxford

[198] British Library reference Add MS 14282 *Berkshire Illustration: Drawings of Ancient Seals* f.8 by B. Howlett 1823. Also see Little 1937 p96

[199] Hurry 1921 p32

[200] Hurry 1901 p37, 132. See also Coates p11, 244 and 261

[201] Gasquet v1 p55

[202] Ibid. p108. This is Article 19

[203] Little 1892 p114; Moorman p91

[204] Hutton p231–235

[205] Gasquet v1 p189–190; Hutton p248; Moorman p92

[206] Gasquet v1 p274–5

[207] Ibid. p289

[208] Ibid. v2 p19 fn

[209] Ibid. p242; Moorman p93–94. See also Little 1892 p115

[210] Moorman p94

[211] Gasquet v1 p461

[212] Little 1892 p117ff

[213] British Library Cleopatra E iv 227; Letters and Papers, Foreign and Domestic, 30 Henry VIII, Volume 13 Part 2 (31 August 1538) 235; Thomas Wright p217f

[214] The Franciscan friaries closed before Reading were: Winchester, Winchelsea, Gloucester, Worcester, Bridgnorth, Lichfield, Stafford, Shrewsbury, Chester, Llanvais, Hereford, Carmarthen, Oxford, Cardiff, Bristol. There is uncertainty about exactly when the Oxford convent was closed (it could have been as early as the first four or five) but the rest are in order of closure, from Winchester on 21 July 1538 to Bristol on 10 September 1538

[215] Coates p303f; Lambeth MSS. 594, fol. 129

[216] The following table gives the information for the Houses where data can be found:

House	Usual no. of friars	No. in 1538/9
Aylesbury	15	7
Cambridge	70	24
Cardiff	18	9
Chichester	26	7
Doncaster	37	10
Dorchester	32	8
Gloucester	40	5
King's Lynn	38	10
Lincoln	50	3
Llanvais	8	4
London	80	26
Northampton	50	11
Oxford	80	18
Reading	13	12

Salisbury	40	10
Stamford	40	10
Winchester	40	3
York	50	16

[217] *A History of the County of Suffolk* Volume 2 in the Victoria County History series (London 1975) p126. This is quoting a letter written on 1 April 1538 by Lord Wentworth of Nettlestead – see Letters and Papers, Foreign and Domestic, 29 Henry VIII, Volume 13 Part 1

[218] Martin p248

[219] Letters and Papers, Foreign and Domestic, 30 Henry VIII, Volume 13 Part 2 (14 September 1538) 346

[220] Ibid. (13 September 1538) 341

[221] Sir John Williams, *Account of the Monastic Treasures confiscated at the Dissolution of the Various Houses in England* (Edinburgh 1836) p13f

[222] British Library Cotton Cleopatra E v; quoted in Coates p304

[223] Summers 2013 p85

[224] British Library Cotton Cleopatra E iv 225; Thomas Wright p222; Coates p304f

[225] Guilding v1 p145

[226] Ibid. p150, 157, 162. See also Coates Appendix XIV. In total, Richard Turner served as mayor seven times, the last two being in 1541–2 (Guilding v1 p176) and 1543–4 (Guilding v1 p185)

[227] British Museum Cotton Manuscript, Cleopatra, E. iv, folio 226; Letters and Papers, Foreign and Domestic, 30 Henry VIII, Volume 13 Part 2 (17th September 1538)

[228] Dictionary of National Biography, 1900, Volume 34

[229] Little 1892 p120

[230] Moorman p97

[231] Letters and Papers, Foreign and Domestic, 31 Henry VIII, Volume 14 Part 2 (20 November 1539) 554

[232] Francis Gasquet, *The Last Abbot of Glastonbury and his Companions: An Historical Sketch* (Simpkin, Marshall, Hamilto & Kent, London 1895) p152

[233] Letters and Papers, Foreign and Domestic, 31 Henry VIII, Volume 14 Part 2 (Undated) 613

[234] In *Notes and Queries Eleventh Series,* Volume X (July–December 1914) (London 1915) Article 10 October 1914 p289, contributor John B. Wainewright states 'One might think the Giles Coventry was "Bachelor Gyles" but that no one of that name is known to have taken a Bachelor's degree'. However, the lists of those friars having taken degrees are known to be incomplete, and we know from Giles Coventry's signature in 1538 that he was styled STB, and thus a Bachelor

[235] George Cornelius Gorham, *Gleanings, or a Few Scattered Ears during the Period of the Reformation in England and of the Times Immediately Succeeding* (Bell and Daldy, London 1857) p466

[236] Giles Coventry is named in a document of 13 February 1611 as a former warden of the dissolved college of Stratford–upon–Avon –see *Shakespeare's birthplace: Catalogue of an Exhibition of Original Documents of the XIVth and XVIIth centuries preserved in Stratford-Upon-Avon* (Edward Fox & Sons, Stratford-upon-Avon 1916) p30. His appointment is given in J. R. Mulryne (Ed.), *The Guild and Guild Buildings of Shakespeare's Stratford: Society, Religion, School and Stage* (Routledge 2016)

[237] A Knight's fee here was £6 13s 4d, that is two thirds of £10. This was the amount of money to provide support for one knight's military service. It was also known as scutage.

[238] Coates p306. See also Letters and Papers, Foreign and Domestic, 31 Henry VIII, Volume 15 p105; Summers 2013 p21–22

[239] Letters and Papers, Foreign and Domestic, 5 Henry VIII Grants in January 1514 item 29; 34 Henry VIII, Volume 18 part 1 p195 Grant 27, items 9 and 19

[240] Berkshire Record Office D/A1/114/115. With thanks to Joan Dils for this reference

[241] Coates p306

[242] Guilding v2 p64

[243] The National Archives Prerogative Court of Canterbury Wills PROB 11/324. The Will of Tanfield Vachel is also partially transcribed in *The Quarterly Journal of the Berks Archaeological and Architectural Society* Volume 3 1893–95, No. 4, p66

[244] *Abstract re Slocombe's Land*, dated 26 May 1862, legal copy in the author's possession

[245] Summers 2013 p53f

[246] Calendar of the Charter Rolls 34 Henry VIII; Grants in April 34 Henry VIII, Letters and Papers, Foreign and Domestic, Henry VIII, Volume 17 (24 April 1542)

[247] See Summers 2013 for the full story

Index

Walter (Fachel) 27
Vansittart, Henry 109
Vastern 6, 109
  Ditch 18, 120

Wales 50, 53, 56
Wallensis, John 82, 83
Walsingham 5
  friary 4, 5, 50, 54, 56, 105
  priory 4
Ware friary 54, 56
Warner 65, 113
Watts, William 81
Waynflete, William 89
Webb, William 108
Weedon, John 110
West Midlands 34
Wilcox, John 77
Willelmus de Abindon 66, 113
Willelmus de Okam 66, 113
William, Brother, warden at
  Reading 71, 72
William of Gainsborough 26
William of Wykeham 88
Williamus de Assewell 66, 113
Wiltshire 71
Winchelsea friary 54, 56, 129
Winchester
  bishop of 10
    Langton, Thomas 71
    Waynflete, William 89
    Wykeham, William of 88
  friary 3, 54, 129

Windes – see Windsor
Windles – see Windsor
Windsor 89, 102
  forest of 12, 19, 20, 30
  Constable of W. Castle 19, 29
  Warden of W. forest 20
Wokingham 30
Wolsey, Thomas 89, 90
Wood, Anthony à 68
Woodman, William 28, 48
Worcester
  bishop of 10
  friary 2, 55, 124, 129
Writtle 88
Wursley, William 71, 113

Yarmouth friary – see Great
  Yarmouth
Yield Hall Place 102
York
  archbishop of 10,
    Wolsey, Thomas 89
  friary 55, 124, 129
Yorkshire 33–35, 56, 93